THE ESSENTIAL
WORLD WAR II
QUIZ BOOK

ALSO BY WILLIAM E. SCOTT

Ground Zero and Beyond: A Reference Guide to the 9/11 Disaster

November 22, 1963: A Reference Guide to the JFK Assassination

The World at War, 1939-1945: A Guide to Facts and Sources

THE ESSENTIAL WORLD WAR II QUIZ BOOK

WILLIAM E. SCOTT

ARCHWAY
PUBLISHING

This book is a work of non-fiction. Unless otherwise noted, the author and the publisher make no explicit guarantees as to the accuracy of the information contained in this book and in some cases, names of people and places have been altered to protect their privacy.

Archway Publishing books may be ordered through booksellers or by contacting:

Archway Publishing
1663 Liberty Drive
Bloomington, IN 47403
www.archwaypublishing.com
1 (888) 242-5904

Because of the dynamic nature of the Internet, any web addresses or links contained in this book may have changed since publication and may no longer be valid. The views expressed in this work are solely those of the author and do not necessarily reflect the views of the publisher, and the publisher hereby disclaims any responsibility for them.

Any people depicted in stock imagery provided by Getty Images are models, and such images are being used for illustrative purposes only. Certain stock imagery © Getty Images.

ISBN: 978-1-4808-8613-1 (sc)
ISBN: 978-1-4808-8615-5 (hc)
ISBN: 978-1-4808-8614-8 (e)

Library of Congress Control Number: 2020902342

Print information available on the last page.

Archway Publishing rev. date: 2/28/2020

In memory of

Vic Morrow
(1929–1982)

and

Rick Jason
(1923–2000)

CONTENTS

ACKNOWLEDGMENTS

I was inspired to publish this book by the courageous and self-effacing young men and women who left their small towns and big cities across the United States to face a world at war. Many volunteered. Many were conscripted. All contributed. Among them were Private Hal Baumgarten, US Army, Lieutenant Commander Laura Cobb, US Navy, Corporal William Dabney, US Army, Sergeant Alexander Drabik, US Army, Lieutenant Mary Harrington, US Navy, Lieutenant Myrtle Brethouwer Hoftiezer, US Army, Corporal Harry Johns, US Army, Private Robert Leckie, US Marine Corps, Lieutenant Leonard Lomell, US Army, Lieutenant Colonel Margaret Ritchie Raffa, US Army Air Force, Lieutenant Colonel Hal Ryder, US Army, Commander Agnes Shurr, US Navy, Corporal E. B. Sledge, US Marine Corps, Colonel James Stewart, US Army Air Force, Lieutenant Karl Timmermann, US Army, and Major Dick Winters, US Army.

During a teaching career that began with Ronald Reagan in the White House and concluded with Barack Obama, I was both fortunate and blessed to have taught many gifted students, including Tony Braithwaite, Steve Calabro, John Connors, Dave Falcone, Jenna Ficchi, Joseph Kain, Katie Karsh, Diana Lim, Jenny Ly, Brian Mann, John Martino, Jackie McBride, John Regan, Jeremy Simon, Robert Sola, Matthew Thomas, Donald Woods, Timothy Wright, and Patrick Zaleski.

For their support and friendship through the years, I would like to acknowledge Thomas Belzer, Father Barry Boyle, SJ, Joseph "Brownie" Brown, Dr. James Burgwyn, Louis Casciato, Eileen Frampton, Jane

Frampton, Steven Ghicondes, Beverly Hadwal, Dr. Thomas Heston, Karen Katrinak, Dennis Kent, Cheryl Thomas Leinheiser, Chuck Longo, Kendall Mattern, Albert Melfi, Father Joseph Michini, SJ, John and Catherine Moore, William and Ella Moore, Rick Orme, Dr. Ben Peters, Daniel Scott (Pa-C, MPAS), Father Frank Skechus, SJ, Father Vince Taggart, SJ, Jerome Taylor, and Kerry Wetzel.

A very special thank you to Mari Preis, who assisted me with editing. The American writer William Arthur Ward said, "The mediocre teacher tells. The good teacher explains. The superior teacher demonstrates. The great teacher inspires." The latter certainly describes my friend Mari. Her commitment to the teaching profession is only exceeded by her dedication and concern for her adoring students. She is without equal.

Finally, to my wife Diane, for allowing me to pursue my passion and for tolerating my eccentricities, thank you.

William E. Scott
Springfield, PA
October 2019

INTRODUCTION

In 2019, the United States, Canada, and the nations of Western Europe commemorated the seventy-fifth anniversary of D-Day, the largest and most complex seaborne invasion in military history. Attending the official ceremonies in Normandy were heads of state, foreign dignitaries, and a dwindling number of soldiers and sailors who participated in the assault. The surviving heroes who made the world safe for democracy are now diminished by the ravages of time, but their memories of that bloody and harrowing day have never wavered.

In the early morning hours of June 6, 1944, after five long years of Nazi domination, a naval force of six thousand warships and lesser craft carried 156,000 American, British, Canadian, and Free French troops across the English Channel and landed them on five predetermined beaches on the coast of France. Their objective: Hitler's *Festung Europa*.

Although meticulously planned down to the last detail, Operation OVERLORD, like most military ventures, was not without its problems. Coalition forces, racked by seasickness and unrelenting fear, were forced to contend with inclement weather, malfunctioning equipment, miscommunication, and the intimidating defenses of Germany's Atlantic Wall—a system of concrete and steel bunkers and fortifications augmented with artillery, machine guns, mortars, and an array of beach obstacles including belts of barbed wire, pressure and radio-controlled mines, and Rommel's asparagus (sharp wooden poles with explosive tips). The prospects of success, especially on Omaha Beach, were anything but guaranteed, and failure was a distinct possibility.

Yet through it all, the grit, determination, and courage exhibited by the citizen-soldier carried the day. By D+1, the Allies had gained control of the designated sectors, securing a precious, yet precarious, foothold on the continent and signaling the beginning of Germany's final collapse.

For the greatest generation, which fought on the plains of Europe and in the jungles of the Pacific, World War II was a seminal moment and a defining event in our nation's history. For the rest of their lives, the valor and sacrifice they exhibited defined who they were and what they represented to their families, friends, and to the world.

Unlike my late uncle, US Airman Joseph Scott, a veteran of the Korean War, I have never served in the armed forces. My military experience has been strictly limited to historical scholarship, but I have always felt a deep and abiding admiration and respect for what the greatest generation accomplished and for the generations that followed in Vietnam, Iraq, Afghanistan, and countless other battlefields.

As a social studies teacher for nearly three decades, first at St. Joseph's Preparatory School in Philadelphia and later at Upper Darby High School in nearby Drexel Hill, it was not only my responsibility to teach the who, what, and where of history, but also to explain *why* the study of history is relevant. According to British historian James Holland, "Remembering the past is vital. It helps us make sense of the present and to prepare for the future. It provides context for today and offers lessons too, for while history does not repeat itself, patterns of human behavior certainly do."

As an ever-growing number of our oldest veterans pass from the scene and first-hand accounts become increasingly scarce, it is crucial that we continue to remember the people, places, and events that made World War II a watershed event. With that thought in mind, I began researching *The Essential World War II Quiz Book* in the spring of 2017. Drawing on a wide variety of sources found in public and university libraries, including hundreds of documentaries, motion pictures, and television programs, I completed the project in a little more than two years.

Unlike my three previous books, which were reference works, this is a compendium of one thousand questions and answers designed to offer the casual student of history, as well as the experienced military enthusiast, a unique perspective on the twentieth century's deadliest war. Carefully written to test the reader's knowledge, the book contains fact-filled and challenging queries about Adolf Hitler and Nazi Germany, military leaders, battles and campaigns, weapons, code-names and nicknames, wartime quotes, military acronyms, GI slang, films, and television programs.

Whatever your level of interest or expertise, I hope that you find *The Essential World War II Quiz Book* both educational and informative and that it will encourage you to delve more deeply into history's most senseless and destructive conflict.

CHAPTER 1
ADOLF HITLER AND NAZI GERMANY

CHAPTER 4.

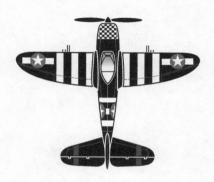

1. Adolf Hitler was born on April 20, 1889, in which Austrian town?

    A. Hallein

    B. Lustenau

    C. Stockerau

    D. Braunau am Inn

2. Hitler was the fourth of _____ children.

    A. five

    B. six

    C. eight

    D. ten

3. Young Hitler was deeply affected when his brother Edmund died in 1900. Which of the following was the cause of death?

    A. Suicide

    B. Cancer

    C. Pneumonia

    D. Measles

4. Which did Hitler's father, Alois, want his son to become when he grew up?

    A. Soldier

    B. Customs official

    C. Farmer

    D. Schoolteacher

5. As a youngster, Hitler served as a(n)

    A. delivery boy

    B. waiter

    C. altar boy

    D. none of the above

6. Hitler was twice rejected from which Austrian art school?

    A. Royal Academy of Arts Salzburg

    B. Academy of Fine Arts Vienna

    C. Fine Arts Institute of Krems

    D. University of Arts and Design Linz

7. Which was the highest level of education attained by Hitler?

    A. Elementary

    B. Secondary

    C. Undergraduate

    D. Postgraduate

8. In 1907, Hitler again suffered a personal loss when his beloved mother died of which ailment?

    A. Pneumonia

    B. Heart failure

    C. Breast cancer

    D. Rheumatic fever

9. Following the death of his mother, Hitler moved to Vienna. He supported himself by

    A. dancing in the streets

    B. playing the violin

    C. working in a bank

    D. painting and selling postcards

10. Prior to the outbreak of World War I, where did Hitler live?

    A. Munich, Germany

    B. Klagenfurt, Austria

    C. Cologne, Germany

    D. Zurich, Switzerland

11. When World War I began, Hitler enlisted in the

    A. Austrian Army

    B. German Army

    C. Bavarian Army

    D. Swiss Army

12. Hitler was wounded at the Battle of (the)

    A. Ypres

    B. Somme

    C. Verdun

    D. Passchendaele

13. Which military decoration did Hitler receive for bravery?

    A. Iron Cross, First Class

    B. Royal Order of Germany

    C. War Merit Cross

    D. Infantry Badge

14. This was the highest military rank achieved by Hitler.

    A. Private

    B. Corporal

    C. Lieutenant

    D. Major

15. Why did Hitler convalesce in a field hospital shortly before the end of the war?

    A. Shrapnel wound

    B. Trench foot

    C. Blinded in a gas attack

    D. Attempted suicide

16. Hitler considered this "the greatest of all experiences."

    A. The First World War

    B. Marrying Eva Braun

    C. Becoming German chancellor

    D. The invasion of Russia

17. Following World War I, Hitler joined which political party?

    A. German Worker's Party (DAP)

    B. Christian Social Party (CSP)

    C. Free Conservative Party (FKP)

    D. German Democratic Party (DDP)

18. Hitler rejected the Treaty of Versailles because it did all of the following *except*

    A. cede colonies to France and Great Britain

    B. impose limitations on naval construction

    C. forbid Germany from having an army

    D. impose significant war reparations

19. Which German journalist and politician became Hitler's mentor in the 1920s?

    A. Joseph Goebbels

    B. Gottfried Feder

    C. Dietrich Eckhart

    D. Anton Federson

20. In _____ the National Socialist German Worker's Party (NSDAP) was formed.

    A. 1919

    B. 1920

    C. 1921

    D. 1922

21. All of the following were charter members of the NSDAP *except*

    A. Anton Drexler

    B. Martin Bormann

    C. Adolf Hitler

    D. Joachim von Ribbentrop

22. Which is the English translation of the NSDAP slogan, *Ein Volk, Ein Reich, Ein Fuhrer*?

    A. "One People, One Nation, One Leader"

    B. "One Voice, One Country, One Leader"

    C. "One People, One Realm, One Leader"

    D. None of the above

23. This German general participated with Hitler in the Munich Beer Hall *Putsch*.

    A. Erich Ludendorff

    B. Karl von Fasbender

    C. Wilhelm Groener

    D. Max von Bahrfeldt

24. While serving time in Landsberg prison, Hitler dictated *Mein Kampf* to

    A. Hermann Goering

    B. Martin Bormann

    C. Rudolf Hess

    D. Albert Speer

25. This was the original title of *Mein Kampf.*

    A. *The Fall of the Established Order and My Role in Bringing It About*

    B. *The Struggle to Save the West from the Mongrel Hoards*

    C. *Why Germany Lost the War*

    D. *Four and a Half Years of Struggle against Lies, Stupidity, and Cowardice*

26. Who persuaded Hitler to change the title of his memoir to *Mein Kampf*?

    A. Emil Maurice

    B. Fritz Wiedemann

    C. Max Amann

    D. Wilhelm Richter

27. The English translation of *Mein Kampf* is

    A. "My Cause"

    B. "My Struggle"

    C. "My Goal"

    D. "My Country"

28. Which political figure found *Mein Kampf* superficial and tedious?

    A. Neville Chamberlain

    B. Charles de Gaulle

    C. Benito Mussolini

    D. Joseph Stalin

29. In the 1920s, Hitler wanted to emulate this European dictator.

    A. Josip Tito

    B. Francisco Franco

    C. Joseph Stalin

    D. Benito Mussolini

30. How many years before the birth of the Nazi Party was the swastika first used?

    A. 1,000

    B. 2,000

    C. 5,000

    D. 10,000

31. The word *swastika* comes from Sanskrit meaning

    A. "love for all"

    B. "peace and joy"

    C. "well-being"

    D. "safe journey"

32. Which German city held the first Nazi rally in 1923?

    A. Cologne

    B. Nuremberg

    C. Hamburg

    D. Munich

33. In 1925, Hermann Goering was treated for severe morphine addiction brought on by a(n)

    A. self-inflicted gunshot wound

    B. back injury from World War I

    C. equestrian mishap

    D. groin injury suffered during the *Putsch*

34. He was a founding member of the *Sturmabteilung*, also known as the "Brownshirts."

    A. Heinz Becker

    B. Otto Paulig

    C. Julius Schreck

    D. Hans Klitzsch

35. Which is the more common name for the *Schutzstaffel*?

    A. SA

    B. SE

    C. SS

    D. SZ

36. This German government spanned from the end of World War I until the ascension of the Nazis.

    A. Berlin Union

    B. Weimar Republic

    C. Hamburg Council

    D. Munich Federation

37. In 1931, Hitler's half-niece, Geli Raubal, allegedly committed suicide in his Munich apartment. Which did authorities say was the cause of death?

    A. Gunshot wound

    B. Drowning

    C. Overdose

    D. Electrocution

38. Who became *Reichstag* president in 1932?

    A. Paul Lobe

    B. Hermann Goering

    C. Max Wallraf

    D. Eduard von Simpson

39. Hitler's dream of creating an economical form of transportation for the masses led to the development of the

    A. Duesenberg Model A

    B. Opel Mokka

    C. Volkswagen Beetle

    D. Adler Trumpf Junior

40. In 1933, a twenty-four-year-old Dutch Communist named _____ was tried, convicted, and executed for setting fire to the German *Reichstag*.

    A. Jan de Hooch

    B. Marinus van der Lubbe

    C. Aldert de Witt

    D. Hans van den Colijn

41. Signed into law by President Paul von Hindenburg, the *Reichstag* Fire Decree did all of the following *except*

    A. suppress media opposition

    B. abolish political organizations

    C. suspend civil liberties

    D. imprison all Jews

42. Who became president of Germany following the death of Hindenburg?

    A. Fredrich Ebert

    B. Ritter von Bernhardt

    C. Hermann Goering

    D. None of the above

43. Like Hitler, he also came to power in 1933.

    A. Benito Mussolini

    B. Franklin Roosevelt

    C. Joseph Stalin

    D. Winston Churchill

44. This statesman served as Weimar chancellor and Nazi vice chancellor.

    A. Franz von Papen

    B. Heinrich Bruning

    C. Joachim von Ribbentrop

    D. Kurt Schmidt

45. University educated and a skilled orator, he carefully crafted the Hitler persona while serving as propaganda minister.

    A.   Gottfried Feder

    B.   Walther Gettner

    C.   Franz Funk

    D.   Joseph Goebbels

46. A veteran of World War I and leader of the *Sturmabteilung* (SA), he was murdered during the "Night of the Long Knives."

    A.   Ernst Rohm

    B.   Otto Wagener

    C.   Viktor Lutze

    D.   Igor von Mueller

47. Before his appointment as head of the SS, Heinrich Himmler was a

    A.   university professor

    B.   chicken farmer

    C.   housepainter

    D.   schoolteacher

48. This was the first concentration camp built in Germany.

    A.   Treblinka

    B.   Dachau

    C.   Auschwitz

    D.   Buchenwald

49. When did the SS take control of the concentration camp system?

    A. 1932

    B. 1934

    C. 1936

    D. 1938

50. Dachau's first SS commandant was

    A. Hans Loritz

    B. Theodor Eicke

    C. Alexander Reiner

    D. Hilmar Wackerle

51. Which SS unit was primarily responsible for overseeing the concentration camps?

    A. "Grenadier"

    B. "Mountain"

    C. "Death's Head"

    D. "Urban Assault"

52. This was the largest Nazi camp for women.

    A. Ravensbruck

    B. Sachsenhausen

    C. Mauthausen

    D. Arbeitsdorf

53. Enacted by the Nazi Party in 1935, they insured the purity of the Aryan race by excluding Jews from German society.

    A. Nuremberg Laws

    B. Dresden Acts

    C. Munich Laws

    D. Leipzig Codes

54. Germany violated the terms of the Versailles Treaty and the Locarno Pact by reoccupying this territory in 1936.

    A. Saarland

    B. Rhineland

    C. Luxembourg

    D. Slovenia

55. This German film producer and director chronicled the Berlin Olympics in the documentary film *Triumph of the Will*.

    A. Claudia Gebbe

    B. Leni Riefenstahl

    C. Doris Dehne

    D. Nina Grossman

56. Which African American shattered Hitler's myth of Aryan superiority by winning four gold medals at the Berlin Olympics?

    A. Ralph Metcalfe

    B. Mack Robinson

    C. Archie Williams

    D. Jesse Owens

57. The Anti-Comintern Pact was an anti-Communist agreement between which two Axis partners?

    A.   Bulgaria and Japan

    B.   Italy and Germany

    C.   Germany and Japan

    D.   Romania and Italy

58. Known for his peculiar remedies and pungent odor, he was the Fuhrer's personal physician for nearly a decade.

    A.   Theodor Morell

    B.   Karl Babor

    C.   Hans Eisele

    D.   Ernst Hefter

59. The name of Hitler's mountaintop retreat in the Bavarian Alps was

    A.   the Berghof

    B.   Versailles

    C.   the Schloss Adler

    D.   Ilsehall

60. Built to honor his late wife, Carinhall was the feudal retreat of which Nazi leader?

    A.   Martin Bormann

    B.   Hermann Goering

    C.   Roland Freisler

    D.   Otto Skorzeny

61. In 1937, Hitler created the Order of the German Eagle for prominent foreigners. All of the following were recipients *except*

    A. John L. Lewis

    B. Henry Ford

    C. Charles Lindbergh

    D. Josip Tito

62. Germany achieved union with Austria in

    A. 1935

    B. 1936

    C. 1937

    D. 1938

63. Which world leader did not sign the Munich Agreement?

    A. Edouard Daladier

    B. Neville Chamberlain

    C. Benito Mussolini

    D. Winston Churchill

64. The murder of a Nazi diplomat by a Polish Jew triggered *Kristallnacht*, a two-day orgy of violence against German Jews. When did *Kristallnacht* take place?

    A. April 3–4, 1938

    B. June 16–17, 1938

    C. October 1–2, 1938

    D. November 9–10, 1938

65. As a result of *Kristallnacht*, some _____ Jewish males were incarcerated.

    A.   10,000

    B.   20,000

    C.   30,000

    D.   40,000

66. *Kristallnacht* means

    A.   "Two Nights of Terror"

    B.   "The Night of Broken Glass"

    C.   "Two Days of Hell"

    D.   "The Night of Horror"

67. Which US publication named Hitler its "Man of the Year" in 1938?

    A.   *Saturday Evening Post*

    B.   *Collier's*

    C.   *Time*

    D.   None of the above

68. A devotee of American cinema, all of the following were Hitler's favorite films *except*

    A.   *King Kong*

    B.   *Dr. Jekyll and Mr. Hyde*

    C.   *Lives of a Bengal Lancer*

    D.   *Snow White and the Seven Dwarfs*

69. Hitler was nominated for which prestigious honor in 1939?

    A.   Fields Medal

    B.   Nobel Prize

    C.   Grammy Award

    D.   Pulitzer Prize

70. This pre-World War II proposal was Hitler's directive to expand Germany's naval forces.

    A.   Plan Green

    B.   Plan X

    C.   Plan White

    D.   Plan Z

71. Issued on August 31, 1939, Fuhrer Directive No. 1 called for

    A.   the extermination of European Jews

    B.   an invasion of England

    C.   the overthrow of the Weimar Republic

    D.   an invasion of Poland

72. Which of the following nations was not part of the Axis alliance?

    A.   Spain

    B.   Germany

    C.   Italy

    D.   Japan

73. Name the German strategy of coordinating air and land forces to rapidly conquer territory.

    A. *Firekrieg*

    B. *Sitzkrieg*

    C. *Blitzkrieg*

    D. *Fritzkrieg*

74. The period between the invasion of Poland and the Battle of France was known as the

    A. Sham War

    B. Fake War

    C. Neutral War

    D. Phony War

75. When Germany invaded the Soviet Union, it violated which agreement?

    A. The Geneva Accords

    B. The Potsdam Agreement

    C. The German-Soviet Non-Aggression Pact

    D. The Treaty of Paris

76. Hitler's decision to attack the Soviet Union was based on the principle of

    A. *Lebensraum*

    B. *Rassenhas*

    C. *Zerstorung*

    D. *Reichtum*

77. Which of the following was not a reason for Hitler's failure to defeat the Soviet Union?

 A. Inability to replenish manpower and equipment

 B. Superiority of Soviet tanks

 C. Poor strategic planning

 D. Failure to utilize tank reserves

78. *Einsatzgruppen* were Nazi mobile units responsible for the murder of

 A. European Jews

 B. French Gaullists

 C. German collaborators

 D. American prisoners of war

79. Which high-ranking Nazi flew to England to negotiate a peace agreement with Great Britain?

 A. Hans Krebs

 B. Oswald Pohl

 C. Rudolf Hess

 D. Arthur Nebe

80. In 1942, German officials convened the _____ Conference to discuss the "Final Solution to the Jewish Question."

 A. Hagen

 B. Wannsee

 C. Aachen

 D. Mannheim

81. This Nazi henchman was Reich Protector of Czechoslovakia and the architect of the Final Solution.

    A.   Bernhard Bosch

    B.   Sepp Mueller

    C.   Henrich Himmler

    D.   Reinhard Heydrich

82. Hitler offered a sizeable bounty to any U-boat captain who could sink this ship:

    A.   RMS *Queen Mary*

    B.   SS *Normandie*

    C.   HMS *Britannic*

    D.   USS *Nevada*

83. As the D-Day landings were taking place, Hitler

    A.   ordered V-2 rocket attacks on the assault beaches

    B.   ate breakfast

    C.   ordered U-boats to attack the Allied armada

    D.   slept

84. Following the Allied invasion of France, Hitler demanded the demolition of which capital?

    A.   Oslo

    B.   Copenhagen

    C.   Brussels

    D.   Paris

85. Where did the July 20, 1944 assassination attempt on Hitler take place?

    A.   Fuhrer's Cove

    B.   Lion's Den

    C.   Wolf's Lair

    D.   Eagle's Nest

86. How many civilian and military leaders took part in the July plot?

    A.   155

    B.   190

    C.   245

    D.   348

87. Which military operation was considered Hitler's final gamble of World War II?

    A.   The mission to rescue Mussolini

    B.   The Battle of the Bulge

    C.   The defense of Berlin

    D.   The invasion of the Soviet Union

88. Name the SS commander whose Panzer unit slaughtered American troops near Malmedy, Belgium.

    A.   Martin Schroif

    B.   Otto Carius

    C.   Joachim Peiper

    D.   Fritz Lang

89. Which Allied power liberated the Auschwitz, Ravensbruck, and Theresienstadt concentration camps?

    A. France

    B. Great Britain

    C. Soviet Union

    D. Canada

90. Along with cyanide, which weapon did Hitler use to commit suicide?

    A. Walther PPK

    B. Luger P08

    C. Mauser C96

    D. Walther P93

91. Why did Hitler choose to end his life?

    A. He felt it was the honorable way to die.

    B. He didn't want the same fate as Mussolini and his mistress.

    C. He wanted to be in control till the very end.

    D. None of the above

92. Name the world leader who died in the same month and year as Hitler.

    A. Joseph Stalin

    B. Gunnar Knudsen

    C. Francisco Franco

    D. Franklin Roosevelt

93. He became leader of the Nazi Party following Hitler's death.

    A. Martin Bormann

    B. Kurt von Schleicher

    C. Roderich Fick

    D. Eugen Fischer

94. Which document, written by the International Military Tribunal, defined the guidelines for the Nuremberg trials?

    A. London Charter

    B. Geneva Charter

    C. Washington Charter

    D. Moscow Charter

95. This British jurist served as the president of the Nuremberg court.

    A. Sir Michael St. John

    B. Hugh Trevor-Roper

    C. Sir Geoffrey Lawrence

    D. Mitchell Redgrave

96. He served as the chief US prosecutor at Nuremberg.

    A. Robert Jackson

    B. Hugo Black

    C. Felix Frankfurter

    D. William O. Douglas

97. In which building were the Nuremberg trials conducted?

    A. Hall of Justice

    B. Palace of Honor

    C. Hall of Mirrors

    D. Palace of Justice

98. Of the twenty-four indicted Nazi defendants, _____ were sentenced to death at Nuremberg.

    A. eight

    B. twelve

    C. nineteen

    D. twenty-four

99. A US Navy deserter, who later joined the US Army, he was the official Nuremberg hangman.

    A. Robert Bailey

    B. John C. Woods

    C. Anthony Rollo

    D. George Venuto

100. Which Nazi leader committed suicide the day before his scheduled execution?

    A. Rudolf Hess

    B. Karl Doenitz

    C. Hermann Goering

    D. Wilhelm Keitel

CHAPTER 1 ANSWERS

1. D. Braunau am Inn

2. B. six

3. D. Measles

4. B. Customs official

5. C. altar boy

6. B. Academy of Fine Arts Vienna

7. B. Secondary

8. C. Breast cancer

9. D. painting and selling postcards

10. A. Munich, Germany

11. C. Bavarian Army

12. B. Somme

13. A. Iron Cross, First Class

14. B. Corporal

15. C. Blinded in a gas attack

16. A. The First World War

17. A. German Worker's Party (DAP)

18. C. forbid Germany from having an army

19. C. Dietrich Eckhart

20. B. 1920

21. D. Joachim von Ribbentrop

22. C. "One People, One Realm, One Leader"

23. A. Erich Ludendorff

24. C. Rudolf Hess

25. D. *Four and a Half Years of Struggle Against Lies, Stupidity, and Cowardice*

26. C. Max Amann

27. B. "My Struggle"

28. C. Benito Mussolini

29. D. Benito Mussolini

30. C. 5,000

31. C. "well-being"

32. D. Munich

33. D. groin injury suffered during the *Putsch*

34. C. Julius Schreck

35. C. SS

36. B. Weimar Republic

37. A. Gunshot wound

38. B. Hermann Goering

39. C. Volkswagen Beetle

40. B. Marinus van der Lubbe

41. D. imprison all Jews

42. D. None of the above

43. B. Franklin Roosevelt

44. A. Franz von Papen

45. D. Joseph Goebbels

46. A. Ernst Rohm

47. B. chicken farmer

48. B. Dachau

49. B. 1934

50. D. Hilmar Wackerle

51. C. "Death's Head"

52. A. Ravensbruck

53. A. Nuremberg Laws

54. B. Rhineland

55. B. Leni Riefenstahl

56. D. Jesse Owens

57. C. Germany and Japan

58. A. Theodor Morell

59. A. the Berghof

60. B. Hermann Goering

61. A. John L. Lewis

62. D. 1938

63. D. Winston Churchill

64. D. November 9–10, 1938

65. C. 30,000

66. B. "The Night of Broken Glass"

67. C. *Time*

68. B. *Dr. Jekyll and Mr. Hyde*

69. B. Nobel Prize

70. D. Plan Z

71. D. an invasion of Poland

72. A. Spain

73. C. *Blitzkrieg*

74. D. Phony War

75. C. The German-Soviet Non-Aggression Pact

76. A. *Lebensraum*

77. D. Failure to utilize tank reserves

78. A. European Jews

79. C. Rudolf Hess

80. B. Wannsee

81. D. Reinhard Heydrich

82. A. RMS *Queen Mary*

83. D. slept

84. D. Paris

85. C. Wolf's Lair

86. B. 190

87. B. The Battle of the Bulge

88. C. Joachim Peiper

89. C. Soviet Union

90. A. Walther PPK

91. B. He didn't want the same fate as Mussolini and his mistress.

92. D. Franklin Roosevelt

93. A. Martin Bormann

94. A. London Charter

95. C. Sir Geoffrey Lawrence

96. A. Robert Jackson

97. D. Palace of Justice

98. B. twelve

99. B. John C. Woods

100. C. Hermann Goering

CHAPTER 2
MILITARY LEADERS

1. This assistant division commander replied, "Nuts!" to the German request for surrender at Bastogne.

    A. Anthony McAuliffe

    B. Maxwell Taylor

    C. Matthew Ridgway

    D. None of the above

2. Admired by General Dwight Eisenhower and feared by Joseph Stalin, he commanded Soviet occupation forces in postwar Germany.

    A. Georgy Zhukov

    B. Konstantin Rokossovosky

    C. Vasily Sokolovsky

    D. Nikita Khruschev

3. Who was the commander of Japanese forces on Iwo Jima?

    A. Minoru Saski

    B. Tadamichi Kuribayashi

    C. Keisuke Fujie

    D. Takeshi Mori

4. Prior to becoming commanding general, European Theater of Operations, which position did Dwight Eisenhower hold?

    A. Army Chief of Staff

    B. Superintendent of West Point

    C. Chief of the War Plans Division

    D. Military aide to FDR

5. This military historian wrote a four-volume biography of US Army General George Marshall.

    A.   Forrest Pogue

    B.   Peter Paret

    C.   Gordon Prange

    D.   Bruce Catton

6. Name the Japanese general who presided at the surrender of American and Filipino forces on Corregidor.

    A.   Seizo Arisue

    B.   Masaharu Homma

    C.   Saburo Hayashi

    D.   Hiroshi Akita

7. All of the following three-star generals were killed during the Second World War *except*

    A.   Millard Harmon

    B.   Frank Andrews

    C.   Simon Buckner

    D.   Anderson Miller

8. The youngest division commander in World War II, he later served as ambassador to France in the Kennedy administration.

    A.   Joseph Collins

    B.   Frederick Browning

    C.   James Gavin

    D.   Leonard Gerow

9. Following the assassination of Admiral Isoroku Yamamoto, _____ became commander-in-chief of the Combined Fleet.

    A. Toshihira Inoguchi

    B. Jinichi Kusaka

    C. Gunichi Mikawa

    D. Mineichi Koga

10. Although he accepted military support from Germany and Italy during the Spanish Civil War, this generalissimo remained primarily neutral during World War II.

    A. Emilio Mola

    B. Miguel Cabanellas

    C. Francisco Franco

    D. Jose Miaja

11. Which German officer was the author of *Infantry Attacks*, a study of military tactics during World War I?

    A. Heinz Guderian

    B. Erwin Rommel

    C. Fritz Becker

    D. Gunther von Kluge

12. This Japanese admiral served as chief of the Imperial General Staff and was against war with the United States and the Soviet Union.

    A. Osami Nagano

    B. Gunichi Mikawa

    C. Dewa Shigeto

    D. Enomoto Takeaki

13. All of the following generals held the five-star rank *except*

    A. Dwight Eisenhower

    B. Henry Arnold

    C. Douglas MacArthur

    D. Courtney Hodges

14. The commanding general of the 1st Ukrainian Front and hero of the Soviet Union, his forces took part in the capture of Berlin in April 1945.

    A. Ivan Konev

    B. Aleksei Brusilov

    C. Valentine Korabelnikov

    D. Anatoly Chernov

15. A graduate of the Imperial Japanese Naval Academy, he led the Pearl Harbor strike force.

    A. Seiichi Ito

    B. Isoroku Yamamoto

    C. Shigeyoshi Inoue

    D. Chuichi Nagumo

16. The following field commanders served as superintendent of the US Military Academy before or after World War II *except*

    A. George Cullum

    B. Frederick Irving

    C. Maxwell Taylor

    D. Bryant Moore

17. He replaced the commanding general of the US II Corps following the Battle of Kasserine Pass.

    A. Lloyd Fredendall

    B. Joseph Stilwell

    C. George Patton

    D. Joseph Webber

18. Known for his administrative skills, he served as deputy military governor of Germany and was responsible for implementing the Berlin Airlift.

    A. Edwin Kelly

    B. Lucius Clay

    C. Dwight Eisenhower

    D. Norman Cota

19. A former educator, _____ went on to command the famed Flying Tigers and is buried in Arlington National Cemetery.

    A. Willis Crittenberger

    B. Claire Chennault

    C. Carl Spaatz

    D. None of the above

20. Which German officer commanded the "Ghost Division" during the invasion of France?

    A. Erwin Rommel

    B. Friedrich Paulus

    C. Erich von Manstein

    D. Gerd von Rundstedt

21. This German naval officer was involved in the planning stages of Operation SEA LION and was subsequently killed in action aboard the battleship *Bismarck*.

    A.   Gunter Luther

    B.   Karl Doenitz

    C.   Gunther Lutjens

    D.   Karl Witzell

22. A member of the Joint Chiefs of Staff, his biography is entitled *Master of Sea Power*.

    A.   Ernest King

    B.   William Leahy

    C.   Chester Nimitz

    D.   Thomas Kinkaid

23. Who was the first commanding general of the US 12th Air Force?

    A.   Hoyt Vandenberg

    B.   Curtis LeMay

    C.   Nathan Twining

    D.   Jimmy Doolittle

24. Considered an energetic and resourceful military leader, he earned a reputation as the "Fuhrer's Fireman."

    A.   Walter Model

    B.   Herman Hoth

    C.   Gunther von Kluge

    D.   Ferdinand Schorner

25. Name the two US admirals killed in action during the First Battle of Guadalcanal.

    A. Frank Fletcher and Thomas Kinkaid

    B. Ronald Brennan and Christopher Sutton

    C. Daniel Callaghan and Norman Scott

    D. Gerald Lockhart and Clark Gormley

26. Who is recognized as the "Father of the *Blitzkrieg*"?

    A. Hasso von Manteuffel

    B. Erwin Rommel

    C. Heinz Guderian

    D. Fedor von Bock

27. He was the commanding officer of the British 8th Army prior to General Bernard Montgomery.

    A. Claude Auchinleck

    B. Alan Cunningham

    C. Neil Ritchie

    D. Richard McCreery

28. These US officers commanded the Army and Navy in Hawaii at the time of the Pearl Harbor attack.

    A. Robert Miller and Johnathan Wainwright

    B. Walter Short and Husband E. Kimmel

    C. Omar Bradley and Walton Walker

    D. Richard Lee and William Halsey

29. Commanding general of the famed 82nd Airborne Division, his autobiography is entitled *On to Berlin*.

    A. Edward Clever

    B. Anthony McAuliffe

    C. Matthew Ridgway

    D. James Gavin

30. Hitler's onetime chauffeur and confidant, he led the 6th Panzer Army during the Battle of the Bulge.

    A. Sepp Dietrich

    B. Kurt Meyer

    C. Paul Hausser

    D. Felix Steiner

31. A graduate of MIT with a doctorate in aeronautical engineering, _____ later received the Medal of Honor for leading the first air raid on Tokyo.

    A. Chuck Yeager

    B. Elwood Quesada

    C. Millard Harmon

    D. Jimmy Doolittle

32. Which air marshal headed RAF fighter command during the Battle of Britain?

    A. Hugh Trenchard

    B. Arthur Tedder

    C. Hugh Dowding

    D. Charles Portal

33. *Crusade in Europe* chronicled the wartime experiences of which high-ranking general?

    A.   George McClellan

    B.   Dwight Eisenhower

    C.   George Marshall

    D.   Jean de Lattre de Tassigny

34. The following held the rank of fleet admiral *except*

    A.   Chester Nimitz

    B.   Marc Mitscher

    C.   William Leahy

    D.   Ernest King

35. A West Point graduate and US Army officer, he organized and commanded the 1st Ranger Battalion. Following his death in 1945, he was posthumously promoted to the rank of brigadier general.

    A.   Mitchell Sutherland

    B.   Lawrence Belford

    C.   William O. Darby

    D.   James Walker

36. Which French officer signed the armistice with Germany near Compiegne, France, on June 22, 1940?

    A.   Charles Huntziger

    B.   Ferdinand Foch

    C.   Maurice Gamelin

    D.   None of the above

37. A veteran of the Pearl Harbor attack, this Japanese admiral was killed in action aboard the carrier *Hiryu* during the Battle of Midway.

    A. Dewa Shigeto

    B. Chiaki Matsuda

    C. Kojuro Nozaki

    D. Tamon Yamaguchi

38. Which member of the German General Staff signed the unconditional surrender document at Reims, France, on May 7, 1945?

    A. Wilhelm Keitel

    B. Alfred Jodl

    C. Karl Uberlitz

    D. Walther von Brauchitsch

39. An outspoken advocate of German naval expansion, he was commander-in-chief of the *Kriegsmarine* until 1943.

    A. Karl Doenitz

    B. Erich Raeder

    C. Wilhelm Brocker

    D. Alfred von Tirpitz

40. This general did not graduate from the US Military Academy.

    A. Mark Clark

    B. John DeWitt

    C. Charles Ryder

    D. Stanley Embick

41. Which of the following admirals did not graduate from the US Naval Academy?

    A. Daniel Barbey

    B. Jeremiah Ford

    C. Robert Carney

    D. Jonas Ingram

42. This air marshal conducted the RAF's strategic bombing campaign against Germany.

    A. Robert Brooke-Popham

    B. Arthur Harris

    C. Roderick Carr

    D. Sholto Douglas

43. He directed the evacuation of Dunkirk and commanded Allied naval forces for the invasion of France.

    A. Dudley Pound

    B. Arthur Cunningham

    C. James Curtis

    D. Bertram Ramsey

44. A brilliant naval tactician, his "Tokyo Express" supplied Japanese troops during the Guadalcanal campaign.

    A. Chuichi Nagumo

    B. Nobutake Kondo

    C. Raizo Tanaka

    D. Isoroku Yamamoto

45. He commanded the US 3rd Army after General George Patton.

    A.   Herbert Brees

    B.   Walter Krueger

    C.   Lucian Truscott

    D.   Courtney Hodges

46. A Luftwaffe fighter ace with 104 confirmed kills, he was appointed *General der Jagdflieger* in 1941. His autobiography is entitled *The First and the Last.*

    A.   Walter Boenicke

    B.   Adolf Galland

    C.   Ernst Buffa

    D.   Wolfgang Erdmann

47. Which serving officer in the British Army formed the special forces unit known as the Chindits?

    A.   Walter Lentaigen

    B.   Archibald Wavell

    C.   Orde Wingate

    D.   Michael Barker

48. Biographer Nigel Hamilton penned a three-volume study of this legendary British officer.

    A.   Bernard Montgomery

    B.   Alan Brooke

    C.   Harold Alexander

    D.   Arthur Percival

49. *American Caesar* was the best-selling biography about this legendary military figure.

    A.   Dwight Eisenhower

    B.   Omar Bradley

    C.   Douglas MacArthur

    D.   Henry Arnold

50. The Soviet Union's most successful military commander, he carried out the defense of Moscow and Stalingrad.

    A.   Dimitri Gorchakov

    B.   Ivan Konev

    C.   Josef Vatutin

    D.   None of the above

51. A Luftwaffe general and veteran of World War I, _____ died as a result of injuries sustained in the assassination attempt on Adolf Hitler.

    A.   Heinz Mueller

    B.   Gunther Korten

    C.   Hans Jeschonnek

    D.   Ritter von Brandt

52. The first Native American to graduate from the US Naval Academy, he commanded Task Group 58 during the Marianas campaign.

    A.   Robert Carney

    B.   Arthur Radford

    C.   Joseph Clark

    D.   Arthur Bristol

53. A member of the famed Richthofen "Flying Circus," he went on to serve as head of procurement for the Luftwaffe before committing suicide in 1941.

   A.   Erhard Milch

   B.   Alfred Sturm

   C.   Werner Anton

   D.   Ernst Udet

54. Who was the first African American general to serve during World War II?

   A.   Vincent Brooks

   B.   Benjamin O. Davis Sr.

   C.   Ronald Bailey

   D.   Benjamin O. Davis Jr.

55. He was the commanding officer of the Japanese 14th Army and was later executed for war crimes relating to the Bataan Death March.

   A.   Tomoyuki Yamashita

   B.   Senjuro Hayashi

   C.   Masaharu Homma

   D.   Torashira Kawabe

56. Known as "the Liberator of Kiev," this Soviet combat commander was mortally wounded by Ukrainian guerilla fighters in 1944.

   A.   Fyodor Tolbukhin

   B.   Andrei Grechko

   C.   Nikolai Vatutin

   D.   Andrey Yeryomenko

57. He was promoted to the rank of *Generalfeldmarschall* by Hitler shortly before surrendering to Soviet forces in Stalingrad.

    A. Wilhelm List

    B. Friedrich Paulus

    C. Kurt Student

    D. Wolfram von Richthofen

58. After surrendering the Philippines in 1942, he became the highest-ranking US general held by the Japanese.

    A. Jonathan Wainwright

    B. Albert Wedemeyer

    C. Mitchell Rodgers

    D. Wade Haislip

59. He commanded the 101st Airborne Division and was later chairman of the Joint Chiefs of Staff.

    A. Lyman Lemnitzer

    B. William Lee

    C. Maxwell Taylor

    D. William Schmidt

60. Chief of the German intelligence service (*Abwehr*), _____ was implicated in the plot to assassinate Hitler and later executed.

    A. Friedrich Ruge

    B. Wilhelm Canaris

    C. Bernhard Rogge

    D. Theodor Krancke

61. The commanding general of the Japanese 32nd Army on Okinawa, he committed ritualistic suicide rather than surrender. Who was he?

    A. Keiji Shibazaki

    B. Mitsuru Ushijima

    C. Yoshitsugu Saito

    D. Tadayoshi Sano

62. Among his many creations was the "DD Tank," which was used during the Normandy invasion.

    A. Evelyn Barker

    B. Percy Hobart

    C. Reginald Beck

    D. Colin Callander

63. Who replaced General Maurice Gamelin as commander-in-chief of French forces during the Battle of France?

    A. Philippe Leclerc

    B. Alphonse Georges

    C. Maxime Weygand

    D. Henri Bouchot

64. This US carrier admiral received his Navy wings at the age of fifty-two.

    A. Mark Mitscher

    B. Barney Giles

    C. William Halsey

    D. John Towers

65. All of the following US commanders served in Europe and the Pacific *except*

    A.   J. Lawton Collins

    B.   Alexander Patch

    C.   Troy Middleton

    D.   Charles Corlett

66. Name the general who led the Polish government-in-exile before his death in an airplane accident.

    A.   Wladyslaw Sikorski

    B.   Leopold Komorowski

    C.   Stanislaw Sosabowski

    D.   Henryk Dobrzanski

67. This US admiral was the subject of naval historian Thomas B. Buell's 1974 biography *The Quiet Warrior*.

    A.   Mitchell Warren

    B.   William Halsey

    C.   Raymond Spruance

    D.   John McCain

68. A Nazi sympathizer and commander-in-chief of Vichy military forces, he was assassinated on Christmas Eve 1942 by a French monarchist.

    A.   Pierre Laval

    B.   Philippe Petain

    C.   Francois Darlan

    D.   Paul Reynaud

69. He was known as the "Father of the U-Boat."

    A. Karl Doenitz

    B. Erich Raeder

    C. Heinz Stuffel

    D. Peter von Bracker

70. Who replaced Admiral James Richardson as commander-in-chief, Pacific Fleet, prior to the Japanese attack on Pearl Harbor?

    A. William Pratt

    B. Joseph Reeves

    C. Frank Schofield

    D. None of the above

71. Name the two US soldiers Patton slapped during the Sicilian campaign.

    A. Charles Kuhl and Paul Bennett

    B. Arthur Wetzel and Homer Rigner

    C. Peter Andrews and George Parsons

    D. John Taylor and Jason Kramer

72. In 1951, he published his best-selling memoir *A Soldier's Story*.

    A. Harold Winston

    B. Omar Bradley

    C. Joseph Stilwell

    D. Claire Chennault

73. Which admiral held the simultaneous titles of commander-in-chief, United States Fleet, and chief of Naval Operations?

    A. Raymond Spruance

    B. Ernest King

    C. Frank Fletcher

    D. Chester Nimitz

74. He was the first commanding general of the US 8th Air Force.

    A. John Curry

    B. Ira Eaker

    C. Frederick Castle

    D. Nathan Bedford Forrest III

75. Whose memoir was entitled *War Diaries, 1939–1945*?

    A. Claude Auckinleck

    B. Keith Park

    C. Alan Brooke

    D. Archibald Wavell

76. This future Japanese admiral lost two fingers on his left hand during the Battle of Tsushima in 1905.

    A. Saigo Judo

    B. Kato Tomosaburo

    C. Isoroku Yamamoto

    D. Akiyama Saneyuki

77. He served as Eisenhower's chief of staff and later as ambassador to the Soviet Union and director of the Central Intelligence Agency.

    A. William Donovan

    B. Harry Butcher

    C. Walter Bedell Smith

    D. Jeremiah Hawley

78. Commander of US Army Ground Forces, he died in a friendly-fire incident in 1944.

    A. Martin Smith

    B. Jacob Devers

    C. Leslie McNair

    D. Warren Jeffries

79. The first Filipino graduate of West Point and the commanding officer of the 41st Infantry Division, he was captured by Japanese forces and allegedly executed in 1944.

    A. Emilio Aguinaldo

    B. Amterio Ricarte

    C. Vincente Lim

    D. Sergio Mabini

80. Known as the "Lion of Verdun," _____ served as chief of state for the Vichy government from 1940 to 1944.

    A. Maxime Weygand

    B. Charles de Gaulle

    C. Henri Giraud

    D. Philippe Petain

81. A general in the Soviet Red Army, he commanded the Western Front during the Battle of Kursk.

    A. Kirill Meretskov

    B. Leonid Govorov

    C. Markian Popov

    D. Vasily Sokolovsky

82. This recipient of a posthumous Medal of Honor was killed aboard his flagship USS *Arizona* during the Pearl Harbor attack.

    A. Isaac Kidd

    B. Warren Chapman

    C. Trevor Morris

    D. Robert Davidson

83. Which German field marshal commanded Army Group Centre during the invasion of the Soviet Union?

    A. Wolfgang Holstein

    B. Ritter von Leeb

    C. Claus Schoener

    D. Fedor von Bock

84. An Annapolis graduate and decorated aviator who captained the US Navy's first escort carrier, he helped plan the Doolittle Raid.

    A. John Hoover

    B. Arthur Radford

    C. Donald Duncan

    D. Jules James

85. The German commander of Nazi-occupied Paris, _____ ignored Hitler's order to destroy the city.

    A.   Hugo Sperrle

    B.   Dietrich von Choltitz

    C.   Erwin Kuemper

    D.   None of the above

86. Name the US Marine Corps general who is often referred to as the "Father of Modern Amphibious Operations."

    A.   George Ellis

    B.   Holland Smith

    C.   Edward Craig

    D.   Oliver Smith

87. Who was the German commander of Army Group South during the invasion of Poland?

    A.   Gerd von Rundstedt

    B.   Wilhelm Milch

    C.   Otto Sultzman

    D.   Friedrich Dollman

88. A US naval officer who served in Europe and the Pacific, he was killed in action during a *kamikaze* attack on his flagship USS *Louisville* in the Philippine Islands.

    A.   James Holloway

    B.   Theodore Chandler

    C.   Henry Mauz Jr.

    D.   Wilson Brown

89. The commanding general of the Services of Supply in the European Theater of Operations, he advocated the desegregation of the US military.

    A. Walter Taylor

    B. Thomas Handy

    C. John Lee

    D. Clifton Monroe

90. As chief of the Army General Staff, he signed the document of surrender for Japan aboard the USS *Missouri*.

    A. Kabayama Sukenari

    B. Heltaro Kimura

    C. Yoshijiro Umezu

    D. Saigo Judo

91. Regarded as the "Father of the American Airborne," this US Army general was instrumental in developing the air plan for the D-Day invasion.

    A. Charles Hall

    B. William Lee

    C. Aaron Daniels

    D. William Schmidt

92. Name the World War I veteran who served as deputy chief of Naval Operations and later as commander of the US 7th Fleet.

    A. Royal Ingersoll

    B. C. Turner Joy

    C. Dudley Knox

    D. Charles Cooke Jr.

93. Who was the Italian commander of Army Group West during the invasion of France?

    A. Francesco de Caprara

    B. Vito Nunziante

    C. Benito Mussolini

    D. Umberto di Savoia

94. A former commander-in-chief, US Fleet, he was commandant of the 14th Naval District in Hawaii on December 7, 1941.

    A. Claude Bloch

    B. Herman Fredericks

    C. Samuel Robison

    D. Richard Leigh

95. Who was the commander-in-chief of the British Expeditionary Force during the Battle of France?

    A. Daniel Beak

    B. Victor Fortune

    C. Allan Adair

    D. John Vereker

96. A West Point graduate and US Army engineer, he became the first person of Hawaiian ethnicity to attain the rank of general.

    A. Neil Richards

    B. Augustus Lu

    C. Henry Kamano

    D. Albert Lyman

97. The following German generals commanded Army Group Vistula before the fall of Berlin *except*

    A.   Heinrich Himmler

    B.   Albert Kesselring

    C.   Gotthard Heinrici

    D.   Kurt von Tippelskirch

98. Who commanded Japanese naval forces at the Battle of the Coral Sea?

    A.   Yukio Seki

    B.   Aritomo Goto

    C.   Shigeyoshi Inoue

    D.   Kiyohide Ozawa

99. A graduate of the US Military Academy, who served with General John J. Pershing in Mexico, he was selected to command the US Army Service Forces in 1942.

    A.   Brehon Somervell

    B.   Eugene Reybold

    C.   Joseph Connors

    D.   Stephen Roberts

100. This cigar-chomping officer was assigned to the XXI Bomber Command in 1944 with the task of developing and executing the air offensive against Japan.

    A.   Billy Mitchell

    B.   Curtis LeMay

    C.   Elwood Quesada

    D.   None of the above

CHAPTER 2 ANSWERS

1. A. Anthony McAuliffe

2. A. Georgy Zhukov

3. B. Tadamichi Kuribayashi

4. C. Chief of the War Plans Division

5. A. Forrest Pogue

6. B. Masaharu Homma

7. D. Anderson Miller

8. C. James Gavin

9. D. Mineichi Koga

10. C. Francisco Franco

11. B. Erwin Rommel

12. A. Osami Nagano

13. D. Courtney Hodges

14. A. Ivan Konev

15. D. Chuichi Nagumo

16. A. George Cullum

17. C. George Patton

18. B. Lucius Clay

19. B. Claire Chennault

20. A. Erwin Rommel

21. C. Gunther Lutjens

22. A. Ernest King

23. D. Jimmy Doolittle

24. A. Walter Model

25. C. Daniel Callahan and Norman Scott

26. C. Heinz Guderian

27. A. Claude Auchinleck

28. B. Walter Short and Husband E. Kimmel

29. D. James Gavin

30. A. Sepp Dietrich

31. D. Jimmy Doolittle

32. C. Hugh Dowding

33. B. Dwight Eisenhower

34. B. Marc Mitscher

35. C. William O. Darby

36. A. Charles Huntziger

37. D. Tamon Yamaguchi

38. B. Alfred Jodl

39. B. Erich Raeder

40. B. John Dewitt

41. B. Jeremiah Ford

42. B. Arthur Harris

43. D. Bertram Ramsey

44. C. Raizo Tanaka

45. C. Lucian Truscott

46. B. Adolf Galland

47. C. Orde Wingate

48. A. Bernard Montgomery

49. C Douglas MacArthur

50. D. None of the above

51. B. Gunther Korten

52. C. Joseph Clark

53. D. Ernst Udet

54. B. Benjamin O Davis Sr.

55. C. Masaharu Homma

56. C. Nikolai Vatutin

57. B. Friedrich Paulus

58. A. Jonathan Wainwright

59. C. Maxwell Taylor

60. B. Wilhelm Canaris

61. B. Mitsuru Ushijima

62. B. Percy Hobart

63. C. Maxime Weygand

64. C. William Halsey

65. C. Troy Middleton

66. A. Wladyslaw Sikorski

67. C. Raymond Spruance

68. C. Francois Darlan

69. A. Karl Doenitz

70. D. None of the above

71. A. Charles Kuhl and Paul Bennett

72. B. Omar Bradley

73. B. Ernest King

74. B. Ira Eaker

75. C. Alan Brooke

76. C. Isoroku Yamamoto

77. C. Walter Bedell Smith

78. C. Leslie McNair

79. C. Vincent Lim

80. D. Philippe Petain

81. D. Vasily Sokolovsky

82. A. Isaac Kidd

83. D. Fedor von Bock

84. C. Donald Duncan

85. B. Dietrich von Choltitz

86. B. Holland Smith

87. A. Gerd von Rundstedt

88. B. Theodore Chandler

89. C. John Lee

90. C. Yoshijiro Umezu

91. B. William Lee

92. D. Charles Cooke Jr.

93. D. Umberto di Savoia

94. A. Claude Bloch

95. D. John Vereker

96. D. Albert Lyman

97. B. Albert Kesselring

98. C. Shigeyoshi Inoue

99. A. Brehon Somervell

100. B. Curtis LeMay

CHAPTER 3
BATTLES AND CAMPAIGNS

1. British military historian John Keegan called it "the most stunning and decisive blow in the history of naval warfare."

    A. Battle of Midway

    B. Battle of the Coral Sea

    C. Battle of Jutland

    D. Battle of Leyte Gulf

2. This was not a reason why Germany lost the Battle of Britain?

    A. British radar allowed for early detection of incoming German aircraft.

    B. Downed RAF pilots were rescued, and Luftwaffe pilots were not.

    C. German strategy shifted from military to civilian targets.

    D. The RAF possessed superior numbers of aircraft.

3. Which of the following battles was fought on American soil?

    A. Jitra

    B. Endau

    C. Attu

    D. Kranji

4. A distinguished professor of history at the US Naval Academy, he is the author of many books, including *The Battle of Midway* and *Neptune: The Allied Invasion of Europe and the D-Day Landings*.

    A. James Bradford

    B. Craig Symonds

    C. Jonathan Parshall

    D. Walter Lord

5. The Battle of Tarawa lasted for _____ days.

    A. two

    B. three

    C. four

    D. six

6. Which US division suffered the heaviest casualties during the Battle of the Hurtgen Forest?

    A. 1st Infantry

    B. 9th Infantry

    C. 28th Infantry

    D. 83rd Infantry

7. On which date did the Japanese air, land, and sea assault on Wake Island begin?

    A. November 11, 1941

    B. December 8, 1941

    C. January 1, 1942

    D. February 15, 1942

8. Where did the "Champagne Campaign" take place?

    A. Eastern Italy

    B. Northern Germany

    C. Eastern Russia

    D. Southern France

9. The Battle of the Coral Sea was considered a

    A. tactical victory for the United States

    B. resounding defeat for Japan

    C. strategic victory for the United States

    D. crushing defeat for the British

10. Prime Minister Winston Churchill called it "the greatest American battle of the war."

    A. Guadalcanal

    B. Anzio

    C. Kasserine Pass

    D. Ardennes

11. The Battle of Iwo Jima began on which date?

    A. March 11, 1943

    B. December 18, 1944

    C. February 19, 1945

    D. None of the above

12. Approximately how many Allied troops took part in the invasion of Sicily?

    A. 80,000

    B. 97,000

    C. 134,000

    D. 150,000

13. On which date did Corregidor fall to the Japanese 14th Army?

    A. January 4, 1942

    B. May 6, 1942

    C. June 12, 1942

    D. August 28, 1942

14. The Battle of Monte Cassino lasted for _____ months.

    A. four

    B. five

    C. six

    D. seven

15. Why was the Battle of the Coral Sea significant?

    A. It was the first naval engagement of World War II.

    B. The Japanese sued for peace.

    C. Neither side lost any ships.

    D. Opposing forces used aircraft to determine the outcome.

16. This political figure was the first to coin the phrase "Battle of Britain."

    A. Winston Churchill

    B. Chiang Kai-shek

    C. Franklin Roosevelt

    D. Adolf Hitler

17. All of the following nations took part in the Burma campaign *except*

    A. the United States

    B. China

    C. Thailand

    D. Poland

18. The Battle of Brody, a German-Soviet tank engagement, was also known as the Battle of

    A. Dubna

    B. Abinski

    C. Stavropol

    D. Brodinski

19. Which battle lasted from April 1, 1945, to June 22, 1945?

    A. Liege

    B. Okinawa

    C. Arnhem

    D. Tarawa

20. A former BBC producer and novelist, he is the author of *The Battle of the Atlantic* and *D-Day to Berlin*.

    A. William Zimmer

    B. Peter Kingsley

    C. George Talbott

    D. Andrew Williams

21. Historians consider this battle the turning point of the Pacific war.

    A. Bismarck Sea

    B. Midway

    C. Savo Island

    D. Coral Sea

22. Which of the following was significant about the Battle of Britain?

    A. It was only fought at night.

    B. Pilots from four different nations took part.

    C. It was the first time a battle was fought entirely in the air.

    D. There were no civilian casualties.

23. Of the 22,000 Japanese troops that defended Iwo Jima, only _____ were captured.

    A. 216

    B. 398

    C. 401

    D. 512

24. How many Allied vessels took part in the D-Day invasion?

    A. 5,082

    B. 6,939

    C. 7,117

    D. 8,238

25. The Battle of Goodenough Island was part of which campaign?

    A.   Mariana Islands

    B.   Wake Island

    C.   Solomon Islands

    D.   New Guinea

26. How many British and French troops were evacuated from Dunkirk?

    A.   175,358

    B.   235,766

    C.   338,226

    D.   None of the above

27. During this naval engagement, Lieutenant Commander Robert Dixon uttered the famous words "Scratch one flattop!"

    A.   Battle of Hampton Roads

    B.   Battle of the Coral Sea

    C.   Battle of Lucas Bend

    D.   Battle of Midway

28. The only country that had a fully mechanized army take part in the Battle of France was

    A.   Belgium

    B.   France

    C.   Germany

    D.   Great Britain

29. Which of the following battles was the costliest of the Pacific war?

    A. Tarawa

    B. Dak To

    C. Okinawa

    D. Ap Gu

30. This titanic clash of armor included some 6,000 German and Soviet tanks.

    A. Battle of Kursk

    B. Battle of Arracourt

    C. Battle of 73 Easting

    D. Battle of Arras

31. Of the following units, which took part in the Battle of Edson's Ridge?

    A. 1st Marine Raiders Battalion

    B. 3rd Army Special Forces Regiment

    C. 9th Marine Raiders Battalion

    D. 21st Army Reconnaissance Group

32. The last naval duel between German and British battleships was the

    A. Battle of Audierne Bay

    B. Battle of the River Plate

    C. Battle of Cape Burnas

    D. Battle of the North Cape

33. During which battle did US Army medic Desmond Doss win the Medal of Honor for conspicuous heroism on Hacksaw Ridge?

    A. Temor

    B. Okinawa

    C. Naples

    D. Verdun

34. Which action occurred last?

    A. Battle of Beda Fomm

    B. Battle of Konigsberg

    C. Battle of Bardia

    D. Battle of Kwajalein

35. American troops were given three objectives at the outset of the Battle of Manila. Which one was not an objective?

    A. Liberate civilians held at the University of Santo Tomas

    B. Reclaim the Malacanan Palace

    C. Liberate the 1,000 POWs held captive in the San Juan de Dios Hospital

    D. Seize the Filipino Congress

36. This was the longest campaign of World War II.

    A. North African

    B. Tunisian

    C. East African

    D. Atlantic

37. In the wartime memoir, *With the Old Breed*, author E. B. Sledge chronicled his experiences during the battles of

    A. Peleliu and Okinawa

    B. Tarawa and Kwajalein

    C. Saipan and Guam

    D. Iwo Jima and Borneo

38. A total of _____ aircraft took part in the Normandy invasion.

    A. 3,560

    B. 4,110

    C. 6,760

    D. 10,440

39. Which of the following US Army divisions participated in the Battle of Buna-Gona?

    A. 78th Infantry

    B. 12th Armored

    C. 32nd Infantry

    D. 2nd Cavalry

40. An award-winning historian and graduate of the Royal Military Academy Sandhurst, Antony Beevor authored this critically acclaimed book in 2018.

    A. *The Battle of Salerno*

    B. *The Battle of Arnhem*

    C. *The Battle of Leningrad*

    D. *The Battle of Bastogne*

41. When did Bataan fall to Japanese forces?

    A. December 30, 1941

    B. January 3, 1942

    C. April 9, 1942

    D. November 12, 1943

42. Of the following battles, which did not take place in Europe?

    A. Pindus

    B. Antietam

    C. Leningrad

    D. Naples

43. A two-term governor from South Dakota and the first commissioner of the American Football League, US Marine Captain Joe Foss was awarded the Medal of Honor for exceptional bravery during this battle.

    A. Pleiku

    B. Leyte Gulf

    C. Guadalcanal

    D. Komar Straits

44. The Battle of Leros was part of which campaign?

    A. East African

    B. Gilbert Islands

    C. Dodecanese

    D. North African

45. During which battle did the Japanese launch the first organized *kamikaze* attacks?

   A. Cape Esperance

   B. Makin

   C. Leyte Gulf

   D. None of the above

46. Which event signaled the end of the Battle of Normandy?

   A. Entrapment of German forces in the Falaise Pocket

   B. Occupation of Merville

   C. Capture of the Orne River Bridge

   D. Liberation of Paris

47. All of the following battles took place in the Pacific *except*

   A. Rabaul

   B. Giarabub

   C. Saipan

   D. Angaur

48. The Battle of _____ was the first major tank engagement of the Second World War.

   A. Libourne

   B. Wroclaw

   C. Hannut

   D. Bytom

49. Which of the following US Marine divisions did not participate in the Battle of Iwo Jima?

    A. 3rd

    B. 4th

    C. 5th

    D. 6th

50. The Battle of Anzio resulted in

    A. the surrender of all German forces in Italy

    B. a seaborne assault on Naples

    C. the liberation of Rome

    D. an airborne assault on Taranto

51. Which battle took place during the Borneo campaign?

    A. Tarakan

    B. Vella Gulf

    C. Garnet Valley

    D. Somerset

52. This system of pillboxes, gun emplacements, and minefields was used to stop the advance of Allied forces during the Battle of Monte Cassino.

    A. Gustav Line

    B. Mussolini Line

    C. Siegfried Line

    D. Augustus Line

53. Which battle occurred first?

    A. Nancy

    B. Coral Sea

    C. San Pietro

    D. El Alamein

54. The Battle of Normandy lasted from

    A. June 3, 1944, to June 18, 1944

    B. June 4, 1944, to July 21, 1944

    C. June 6, 1944, to August 25, 1944

    D. June 7, 1944, to September 1, 1944

55. Which of the following battles took place during the Gilbert Islands campaign?

    A. Manado

    B. Palembang

    C. Toomar

    D. None of the above

56. An American historian and Pulitzer Prize-winning writer, John Toland was the author of several books, including

    A. *Battle: The Story of the Bulge*

    B. *The Battle of Britain*

    C. *At Dawn We Slept*

    D. *Day of Infamy*

57. The Battle of _____ was the first example of urban warfare during the Pacific war.

    A. Pusan

    B. Corregidor

    C. Truk

    D. Manila

58. Great Britain's first ground victory against German forces came at the

    A. Battle of Morocco

    B. Battle of El Alamein

    C. Battle of Mechili

    D. Battle of Bardia

59. The Battle of Eniwetok was significant for all of the following reasons *except*

    A. The atoll became a military base for US forces.

    B. Most of the Japanese defenders capitulated.

    C. The atoll became a launch site for future operations.

    D. US forces suffered relatively few casualties.

60. Where did the Canadian 3rd Infantry Division land on D-Day?

    A. JUNO Beach

    B. UTAH Beach

    C. TIGER Beach

    D. SILVER Beach

61. During which naval action was the US aircraft carrier *Yorktown* sunk?

    A. Battle of the Philippine Sea

    B. Battle of Guadalcanal

    C. Battle of Midway

    D. Battle of the Java Sea

62. Known for his popular studies of World War II, this Irish war correspondent and journalist was the author of *The Longest Day* and *The Last Battle*.

    A. Bennett Johnston

    B. Cornelius Ryan

    C. William L. Shirer

    D. Peter Bartholomew

63. The lessons learned from the Battle of _____ prepared the Allies for future operations in the Central Pacific.

    A. Saipan

    B. Guam

    C. New Caledonia

    D. Tarawa

64. Which was the name of the promontory that US Army Rangers assaulted on D-Day?

    A. Sagres

    B. Pointe du Hoc

    C. Etretat

    D. Pointe du Mere

65. The Battle of Kwajalein taught the Japanese that

    A. poison gas was necessary

    B. beachline defense was ineffective

    C. they could not defeat the Allies

    D. *Banzai* charges were impractical

66. Where did the Germans expect the Allied invasion of Europe to take place?

    A. Corsica

    B. Normandy

    C. Marseille

    D. Pas-de-Calais

67. The following battles were part of America's "island hopping" strategy *except*

    A. Inchon

    B. Tarawa

    C. Kwajalein

    D. None of the above

68. A serving officer in the British Army during World War II, he is the author of *The Battle of El Alamein* and *The Battle of Monte Cassino.*

    A. Glyn Harper

    B. Niall Bar

    C. Ken Ford

    D. Fred Majdalany

69. Which of the following engagements took place during the Dutch East Indies campaign?

    A. Battle of Trikei

    B. Battle of Dunado

    C. Battle of Balikpapan

    D. Battle of Romar

70. On which beaches did British troops land on D-Day?

    A. NEPTUNE and TIGER

    B. SWORD and JUNO

    C. GOLD and SWORD

    D. SILVER and BRONZE

71. Which island battle featured Hill 362 and Hill 382?

    A. Sicily

    B. Iwo Jima

    C. Tarawa

    D. Honshu

72. This was a key action in the Allied drive to the German Siegfried Line.

    A. Battle of Hill 104

    B. Battle of Culp's Hill

    C. Battle of Hill 616

    D. Battle of Crucifix Hill

73. When did the Second Battle of Guam occur?

    A. February 3, 1943, to June 5, 1943

    B. July 21, 1944, to August 10, 1944

    C. September 6, 1944, to November 22, 1944

    D. January 7, 1945, to March 18, 1945

74. During which campaign did the Battle of Morava-Ivan take place?

    A. Balkans

    B. North African

    C. Burma

    D. East African

75. The Medal of Honor was awarded to _____ US military personnel who fought in the Battle of Iwo Jima.

    A. twelve

    B. sixteen

    C. twenty-one

    D. twenty-seven

76. Which iconic structure survived the Battle of Britain, serving as an inspiration to the English people?

    A. St. Alban's Church

    B. Inner Temple Library

    C. St. Paul's Cathedral

    D. Great Synagogue of London

77. A former US naval officer who served in Vietnam, Thomas Cutler was a professor of history at Annapolis and the founder of the Walbrook Maritime Academy. He is the author of several books, including

 A. *The Battle of Leyte Gulf*

 B. *Miracle at Midway*

 C. *The Battle of the Philippine Sea*

 D. *Operation Downfall*

78. Name the war correspondent who first coined the phrase "Battle of the Bulge."

 A. Larry Newman

 B. James Aldridge

 C. Walter Cronkite

 D. Hank Gorrell

79. Which Pacific battle included intense fighting on Purple Heart Ridge?

 A. Java Sea

 B. Wake Island

 C. Jutland

 D. Saipan

80. How many total casualties resulted from the Battle of Normandy?

 A. 60,000

 B. 150,000

 C. 400,000

 D. 520,000

81. During which naval clash was the aircraft carrier USS *Hornet* sunk?

    A. Battle of the Denmark Strait

    B. Battle of the Falkland Islands

    C. Battle of Taranto

    D. Battle of the Santa Cruz Islands

82. In which country did the Battle of Gazala take place?

    A. Egypt

    B. Tunisia

    C. Algeria

    D. Libya

83. A former staff writer for CBS News and novelist, George Feifer is the author of the 2011 bestseller

    A. *The Battle of Okinawa*

    B. *Alamein: Blood in the Desert*

    C. *The Day of Battle*

    D. *Stalingrad: War of Steel*

84. In which North African country was the Battle of Hill 609 fought?

    A. Tunisia

    B. Morocco

    C. Algeria

    D. Sudan

85. The Battle of Makin was part of which Pacific campaign?

    A. Mariana Islands

    B. Admiralty Islands

    C. Gilbert Islands

    D. Aleutian Islands

86. What was the first tank engagement won by the Italians?

    A. Battle of Bir el Gubi

    B. Battle of Hadi bu

    C. Battle of Qalansiyah

    D. Battle of Sidi Bou Jid

87. Name the four Japanese aircraft carriers that were sunk during the Battle of Midway.

    A. *Hosho*, *Kaiyo*, *Hiryu*, and *Zuikaku*

    B. *Kaga*, *Unyo*, *Taiyo*, and *Shokaku*

    C. *Akagi*, *Kaga*, *Soryu*, and *Hiryu*

    D. *Hiryu*, *Amagi*, *Hiryu*, and *Katsuragi*

88. Douglas Nash is a former US Army officer and graduate of West Point. He is the author of *Hell's Gate*, a book about the little-known Battle of the

    A. Lypovec Salient

    B. Hanko Pass

    C. Smolensk Valley

    D. Cherkassy Pocket

89. A veteran of the Doolittle Raid and the Battle of Midway, she was torpedoed and sunk during the Battle of Santa Cruz Islands.

    A. USS *Wasp*

    B. USS *Ticonderoga*

    C. USS *Enterprise*

    D. None of the above

90. The American defense of _____ contributed to the collapse of Germany's Ardennes offensive.

    A. Brussels

    B. St. Vith

    C. Bastogne

    D. Ghent

91. On which date did US land, air, and sea forces assault the island of Saipan?

    A. April 1, 1944

    B. May 23, 1944

    C. June 15, 1944

    D. August 10, 1944

92. Approximately how many Soviet civilians were killed during the Battle of Stalingrad?

    A. 15,000

    B. 20,000

    C. 35,000

    D. 40,000

93. During which battle did Japanese civilians and soldiers commit mass suicide by jumping from Banzai Cliff?

    A. Tinian

    B. Luzon

    C. Saipan

    D. Honshu

94. Which operation signaled the beginning of the Italian campaign?

    A. The Allied landings at Salerno

    B. The bombing of Monte Cassino

    C. The British airborne assault on Sorento

    D. The sinking of the Italian battleship *Roma*

95. How many noncombat casualties did the US 6th Army suffer in the Battle of Luzon?

    A. 67,000

    B. 82,000

    C. 93,000

    D. 102,000

96. Why was the Battle of Stalingrad significant?

    A. It was Germany's first victory against Soviet forces.

    B. It was the final battle on the Eastern Front.

    C. It was the only time a German field marshal committed suicide.

    D. It was Germany's first major defeat.

97. During which naval clash was the tactic known as "capping the T" utilized?

    A. Battle of Mobile Bay

    B. Battle of Surigao Strait

    C. Battle of Gababutu

    D. Battle of Cam Ranh Bay

98. In which country was the Battle of Crete fought?

    A. Monaco

    B. Greece

    C. Malta

    D. Portugal

99. The Battle of Kolombangara took place in which Pacific island chain?

    A. Solomons

    B. Marianas

    C. Aleutians

    D. Marshalls

100. It was during this battle that English-speaking Germans masqueraded as American GIs.

    A. Ypres

    B. Messines

    C. Ardennes

    D. Berlin

CHAPTER 3 ANSWERS

1. A. Battle of Midway

2. D. The RAF possessed superior numbers of aircraft.

3. C. Attu

4. B. Craig Symonds

5. C. four

6. C. 28th Division

7. B. December 8, 1941

8. D. Southern France

9. C. strategic victory for the United States

10. D. Ardennes

11. C. February 19, 1945

12. D. 150,000

13. B. May 6, 1942

14. A. four

15. D. Opposing forces used aircraft to determine the outcome.

16. A. Winston Churchill

17. D. Poland

18. A. Dubna

19. B. Okinawa

20. D. Andrew Williams

21. B. Midway

22. C. It was the first time a battle was fought entirely in the air.

23. A. 216

24. B. 6,939

25. D. New Guinea

26. C. 338,226

27. B. Battle of the Coral Sea

28. D. Great Britain

29. C. Okinawa

30. A. Battle of Kursk

31. A. 1st Marine Raiders Battalion

32. D. Battle of the North Cape

33. B. Okinawa

34. B. Battle of Konigsberg

35. C. Liberate the 1,000 POWs held captive in the San Juan de Dios Hospital

36. D. Atlantic

37. A. Peleliu and Okinawa

38. D. 10,440

39. C. 32nd Infantry

40. B. *The Battle of Arnhem*

41. C. April 9, 1942

42. B. Antietam

43. C. Guadalcanal

44. C. Dodecanese

45. C. Leyte Gulf

46. D. Liberation of Paris

47. B. Giarabub

48. C. Hannut

49. D. 6th

50. C. the liberation of Rome

51. A. Tarakan

52. A. Gustav Line

53. B. Coral Sea

54. C. June 6, 1944, to August 25, 1944

55. D. None of the above

56. A. *Battle: The Story of the Bulge*

57. D. Manila

58. B. Battle of El Alamein

59. B. Most of the Japanese defenders capitulated.

60. A. JUNO Beach

61. C. Battle of Midway

62. B. Cornelius Ryan

63. D. Tarawa

64. B. Pointe du Hoc

65. B. beachline defense was ineffective.

66. D. Pas-de-Calais

67. A. Inchon

68. D. Fred Majdalany

69. C. Battle of Balikpapan

70. C. GOLD and SWORD

71. B. Iwo Jima

72. D. Battle of Crucifix Hill

73. B. July 21, 1944, to August 10, 1944

74. A. Balkans

75. D. twenty-seven

76. C. St. Paul's Cathedral

77. A. *The Battle of Leyte Gulf*

78. A. Larry Newman

79. D. Saipan

80. C. 400,000

81. D. Battle of the Santa Cruz Islands

82. D. Libya

83. A. *The Battle of Okinawa*

84. A. Tunisia

85. C. Gilbert Islands

86. A. Battle of Bir el Gubi

87. C. *Akagi, Kaga, Soryu,* and *Hiryu*

88. D. Cherkassy Pocket

89. D. None of the above

90. C. Bastogne

91. C. June 15, 1944

92. D. 40,000

93. C. Saipan

94. A. The Allied landings at Salerno

95. C. 93,000

96. D. It was Germany's first major defeat.

97. B. Battle of Surigao Strait

98. B. Greece

99. A. Solomons

100. C. Ardennes

CHAPTER 4
WEAPONS

1. Following the Pearl Harbor disaster, the _____ became the dominant weapon of the Pacific war.

    A. submarine

    B. atomic bomb

    C. heavy cruiser

    D. aircraft carrier

2. Which was the main armament on a *Panzerkampfwagen Tiger Ausf. E*?

    A. 60 mm

    B. 75 mm

    C. 88 mm

    D. 90 mm

3. How many Allied aircraft were lost during "Big Week"?

    A. 175

    B. 274

    C. 385

    D. 411

4. Which was the crew capacity of the Japanese Mitsubishi Ki-213 twin-engine bomber?

    A. Five

    B. Eight

    C. Ten

    D. Twelve

5. An American heavy bomber, it was mass-produced at Willow Run in Ypsilanti, Michigan.

    A. B-17 Flying Fortress

    B. B-24 Liberator

    C. B-29 Superfortress

    D. None of the above

6. The standard rifle of the Italian Army, it was also the weapon used in the assassination of President John F. Kennedy.

    A. Beretta 38A

    B. Carcano Modello 1891

    C. Breda Modello 30

    D. Vetterli M1870

7. Which of the following was not a United States Navy (USN) *Iowa*-class battleship?

    A. USS *Pennsylvania*

    B. USS *New Jersey*

    C. USS *Wisconsin*

    D. USS *Missouri*

8. How many .50 caliber machine guns were on a B-17G?

    A. Eight

    B. Thirteen

    C. Ten

    D. Twelve

9. A German surface raider, it was scuttled in South American waters by Captain Hans Langsdorff in 1939.

    A. *Richard Beitzen*

    B. *Hessen*

    C. *Leipzig*

    D. *Admiral Graf Spee*

10. Which of the following was not a Flying Tigers squadron?

    A. "Panda Bears"

    B. "Damn Yankees"

    C. "Hell's Angels"

    D. "Adam and Eves"

11. Germany began using the V-1 flying bomb against Great Britain on

    A. September 1, 1939

    B. July 2, 1942

    C. June 13, 1944

    D. April 29, 1945

12. American industrialist Henry Kaiser is best remembered for mass-producing which type of vessel?

    A. Destroyers

    B. Liberty ships

    C. Minesweepers

    D. Heavy cruisers

13. How many aircraft carriers did the Japanese use for the Pearl Harbor operation?

    A. Five

    B. Seven

    C. Eight

    D. Six

14. The _____ was the most expensive US fighter produced during the war.

    A. P-38 Lightning

    B. P-40 Warhawk

    C. P-47 Thunderbolt

    D. P-51 Mustang

15. Which type of aircraft was the Italian Ambrosini SAI 403?

    A. Trainer

    B. Fighter

    C. Bomber

    D. Glider

16. The following were Imperial Japanese Navy (IJN) *Kuma*-class light cruisers *except*

    A. the *Tama*

    B. the *Kiso*

    C. the *Kitakami*

    D. the *Yaku*

17. General George Patton called it "the greatest battle implement ever devised."

    A. Sherman tank

    B. Ka-Bar knife

    C. M-1 Garand rifle

    D. M1911 pistol

18. All of the following aircraft took part in the Battle of Britain *except*

    A. the Hurricane MK I

    B. the Spitfire MK I

    C. the Tempest MK II

    D. the Messerschmitt Bf 109E

19. Which Japanese submarine sank the USS *Indianapolis*?

    A. I-21

    B. I-58

    C. I-67

    D. I-88

20. The German *Panzerfaust* was used most effectively against

    A. aircraft

    B. tanks

    C. infantry

    D. None of the above

21. Which was the average crew capacity of a B-29?

    A. Ten

    B. Eleven

    C. Twelve

    D. Sixteen

22. It was Germany's most effective "tank-killer" on the Eastern Front.

    A. *Panzerkampwagen* III

    B. *Sturmgeschutz* III

    C. *Panzerfeldhaubitze* 18M

    D. *Sonderkraftfahrzeug* 6

23. This aircraft manufacturer produced the British Hurricane fighter.

    A. Supermarine

    B. Hawker Aircraft

    C. Havilland Aircraft Company

    D. Gloster Aircraft Company

24. All of the following were IJN *Mogami*-class heavy cruisers *except*

    A. the *Mikuma*

    B. the *Suzuya*

    C. the *Kumano*

    D. the *Daito*

25. How many engines did the B-25 Mitchell bomber have?

    A. One

    B. Four

    C. Three

    D. Two

26. Commonly known as the "Higgins Boat," this craft was constructed primarily from which type of material?

    A. Steel

    B. Fiberglass

    C. Plywood

    D. Titanium

27. This American manufacturer produced the SBD Dauntless.

    A. Consolidated Aircraft

    B. Grumman

    C. Douglas Aircraft

    D. Lockheed

28. Which was the normal bomb capacity of a B-24 Liberator?

    A. 8,000 lbs.

    B. 12,800 lbs.

    C. 11,500 lbs.

    D. 13,000 lbs.

29. Considered the most powerful cannon ever produced, the German "Gustav" railway gun could fire a projectile _____ miles.

    A. fifteen

    B. thirty

    C. forty-five

    D. seventy

30. Also known as "jeep carriers" or "baby flattops," USN *Bogue*-class carriers deployed approximately how many aircraft?

    A. Thirty-five

    B. Fifteen

    C. Twenty-four

    D. Ten

31. This was the primary function of the US 15th Air Force.

    A. Provide air defense for the Eastern United States

    B. Conduct operations during the D-Day invasion

    C. Provide air defense for the Hawaiian Islands

    D. Bomb targets in France and Germany

32. Which was the home base of the US 8th Air Force?

    A. England

    B. China

    C. Italy

    D. Spain

33. The HMS *Prince of Wales* and HMS *Repulse* were sunk by Japanese aircraft on

    A. February 22, 1940

    B. October 14, 1940

    C. December 10, 1941

    D. January 8, 1942

34. Which US bomber was mass-produced in greater numbers?

    A. B-17 Flying Fortress

    B. B-24 Liberator

    C. B-25 Mitchell

    D. B-29 Superfortress

35. This version of the Lee-Enfield rifle became the standard issue weapon of the British Army in 1941.

    A. No. 4 MK I

    B. ZB 26

    C. No. 6 MK II

    D. BK 5

36. Which was the crew capacity of a US M3 Stuart tank?

    A. Four

    B. Three

    C. Five

    D. Six

37. The battleship *Yamato's* main battery consisted of _____ 18-inch guns.

    A. six

    B. nine

    C. twelve

    D. None of the above

38. Which US company manufactured the B-24 Liberator?

    A. Boeing

    B. Consolidated Aircraft

    C. North American Aviation

    D. Glenn L. Martin Company

39. All of the following were IJN *Fubuki*-class destroyers *except*

    A. the *Miyuki*

    B. the *Hato*

    C. the *Isonami*

    D. the *Uranami*

40. Produced in 1943, it was arguably the best German tank of World War II.

    A. Tiger I

    B. Panther

    C. Tiger II

    D. Jaguar

41. Which type of aircraft was used to shoot down the transport bomber carrying Admiral Yamamoto on April 18, 1943?

    A.   P-47 Thunderbolt

    B.   F6F Hellcat

    C.   P-38 Lightning

    D.   F4F Wildcat

42. This was the first British ship lost to a U-boat.

    A.   HMS *Athenia*

    B.   HMS *Coventry*

    C.   HMS *Ark Royal*

    D.   HMS *Manchester*

43. Which of the following was the major drawback to the M3 Lee tank?

    A.   Poor acceleration

    B.   Inadequate side armor

    C.   Lack of firepower

    D.   Non-traversing front turret

44. On which US battleship did twenty-three sets of brothers perish on December 7, 1941?

    A.   USS *Oklahoma*

    B.   USS *Nevada*

    C.   USS *Arizona*

    D.   USS *West Virginia*

45. General George Marshall called it "America's greatest contribution to modern warfare."

    A. Bazooka

    B. Half-track

    C. Willys jeep

    D. carbine

46. The following plants manufactured the B-29 *except*

    A. Boeing, Seattle, Washington

    B. Glenn Martin, Omaha, Nebraska

    C. Bell Aircraft, Atlanta, Georgia

    D. Hudson, Camden, New Jersey

47. Of the following aircraft, which had the highest maximum speed?

    A. P-40 Warhawk

    B. P-47 Thunderbolt

    C. P-51 Mustang

    D. P-38 Lightning

48. Which ship was not a USN *Fletcher*-class destroyer?

    A. USS *Quincy*

    B. USS *Radford*

    C. USS *Jenkins*

    D. USS *Sigsbee*

49. Designed to replace the M4 Sherman tank, the M26 Pershing was first deployed to the European Theater in

    A. July 1942

    B. May 1943

    C. December 1944

    D. February 1945

50. Which reporter gave the B-17 Flying Fortress its iconic name?

    A. Ernie Pyle

    B. Marguerite Higgins

    C. Richard L. Williams

    D. Edward R. Murrow

51. The following were USN *Essex*-class aircraft carriers *except*

    A. the USS *Intrepid*

    B. the USS *Franklin*

    C. the USS *Ticonderoga*

    D. the USS *Porter*

52. Also known as the *Schwalbe*, the ME-262 jet fighter first saw combat in

    A. 1942

    B. 1943

    C. 1944

    D. 1945

53. Which US torpedo was plagued by various malfunctions during the early stages of the war?

    A.   Mark 5

    B.   Mark 8

    C.   Mark 10

    D.   Mark 14

54. A British invention, the "Churchill Crocodile" was a(n)

    A.   flame-throwing tank

    B.   underwater half-track

    C.   minelaying tank

    D.   floating bulldozer

55. Which of the following was not a USN *Baltimore*-class heavy cruiser?

    A.   USS *Canberra*

    B.   USS *Pittsburgh*

    C.   USS *Tripoli*

    D.   USS *Columbus*

56. The _____ was the most widely used troop/cargo glider of the Second World War.

    A.   Waco CG-4

    B.   Antonio A-7

    C.   Devonshire X-1

    D.   None of the above

57. *Bismarck*'s sister ship was named

    A.   the *Gneisenau*

    B.   the *Prince Eugen*

    C.   the *Scharnhorst*

    D.   the *Tirpitz*

58. Which was not a USN *Casablanca*-class escort carrier?

    A.   USS *Bougainville*

    B.   USS *Mission Bay*

    C.   USS *St. Paul*

    D.   USS *Guadalcanal*

59. The M4 Sherman was developed to replace which tank?

    A.   M3 Lee

    B.   M24 Chaffee

    C.   Stuart

    D.   M26 Pershing

60. Which weapon proved most effective against Japanese fortifications on Iwo Jima?

    A.   Hand grenades

    B.   Flamethrowers

    C.   Satchel charges

    D.   All of the above

61. This type of aircraft was flown by the RAF's 617 "Dambusters" Squadron.

    A. Vickers Wellesley

    B. Avro Lancaster

    C. Bristol Beaufort

    D. Vickers Wellington

62. How many Japanese planes were used in the attack on Pearl Harbor?

    A. 250

    B. 353

    C. 408

    D. 536

63. The Tuskegee Airmen flew which fighter aircraft?

    A. P-51 Mustang

    B. B-23 Jupiter

    C. F6F Hellcat

    D. P-38 Lightning

64. Approximately how many Japanese warplanes were lost during the Great Marianas Turkey Shoot?

    A. 200

    B. 300

    C. 500

    D. 600

65. Which production model of the B-17 featured the Bendix chin turret?

    A. B

    B. C

    C. G

    D. J

66. On which date was the USS *Indianapolis* torpedoed and sunk?

    A. December 7, 1941

    B. June 12, 1942

    C. August 16, 1944

    D. July 30, 1945

67. The main armament on the US M7 Priest self-propelled howitzer was the

    A. 75 mm

    B. 88 mm

    C. 90 mm

    D. 105 mm

68. Which type of aircraft was the Soviet Yakovlev Yak-3?

    A. Floatplane

    B. Twin-engine bomber

    C. Single-engine fighter

    D. Glider

69. This bomber was used in the Doolittle Raid on Tokyo.

    A. B-17 Flying Fortress

    B. B-24 Liberator

    C. B-25 Mitchell

    D. B-32 Intruder

70. Germany's first diesel-electric U-boat was

    A. the Type XVI

    B. the Type XXI

    C. the Type XXV

    D. the Type XXX

71. Which US carrier-based torpedo bomber replaced the TBD Devastator in 1942?

    A. F4U Corsair

    B. SB2U Vindicator

    C. TBF Avenger

    D. SB2C Helldiver

72. This was the standard infantry rifle of the German *Wehrmacht*.

    A. *Gewehr* 41M

    B. *Volkssturmgewehr* 1

    C. *Karabiner* 98K

    D. *Sturmgewehr* 44

73. Which was the maximum speed of the Japanese Kawasaki Ki-100 fighter?

    A. 295 mph

    B. 360 mph

    C. 405 mph

    D. 515 mph

74. This was the first US warship torpedoed and sunk by a U-boat.

    A. USS *Helena*

    B. USS *Walker*

    C. USS *Greer*

    D. USS *Reuben James*

75. How many sister ships did the German cruiser *Admiral Scheer* have?

    A. Zero

    B. Two

    C. Three

    D. Four

76. The Flying Tigers flew which of the following aircraft?

    A. P-39 Airacobra

    B. P-51 Mustang

    C. P-40 Warhawk

    D. P-46 Shark

77. Approximately how many M4 Sherman tanks were mass-produced between 1942 and 1945?

   A. 20,000

   B. 40,000

   C. 50,000

   D. 70,000

78. On which US warship were the five Sullivan brothers killed on November 13, 1942?

   A. USS *Juneau*

   B. USS *Peterson*

   C. USS *Argonne*

   D. USS *Valley Forge*

79. This German tank destroyer first saw action during the Battle of Kursk.

   A. Napoleon

   B. Panther

   C. Ferdinand

   D. Leopard

80. Which US aviation company manufactured the F4F Wildcat?

   A. Bell Aircraft

   B. Republic Aviation

   C. North American Aviation

   D. Grumman Aircraft

81. The M1A1 Thompson could fire this many rounds per minute.

    A. 100

    B. 300

    C. 500

    D. 700

82. How many Japanese aircraft carriers were sunk during the Battle of Leyte Gulf?

    A. Three

    B. Four

    C. Five

    D. Seven

83. This country used the Norden bombsight to enhance its daylight bombing strategy.

    A. Soviet Union

    B. France

    C. United States

    D. Germany

84. Which Japanese warplane was manufactured by the Aichi Aircraft Company?

    A. E16A1 seaplane

    B. P1Y medium bomber

    C. A6M single-engine fighter

    D. T6A four-engine bomber

85. A British military engineer, he invented the "Tall Boy" and "Grand Slam" bombs for the RAF.

    A. Barnes Wallis

    B. Jacob Nolan

    C. Benjamin Conroy

    D. Roger Smiley

86. No match for Allied armor, it was still considered the finest Japanese medium tank of World War II.

    A. Type 3 Chi-Nu

    B. Type 87 Chi-1

    C. Type 89 Chi-Ro

    D. Type 97 Chi-Ra

87. This was the preferred weapon of US Rangers and British commandos.

    A. M1 carbine

    B. Karabiner 98K

    C. M1903 Springfield

    D. M1A1 Thompson

88. How many Japanese aircraft were destroyed during the Pearl Harbor attack?

    A. Eighteen

    B. Twenty-nine

    C. Thirty-six

    D. Forty-two

89. Approximately how many T-34 tanks did the Soviets produce during the war?

    A. 30,000

    B. 50,000

    C. 80,000

    D. 100,000

90. Which of the following was not a USN *Brooklyn*-class light cruiser?

    A. USS *Gladwyn*

    B. USS *Philadelphia*

    C. USS *Savannah*

    D. USS *Nashville*

91. Developed during World War I, this French light tank saw action in the Spanish Civil War and against Axis forces in the early stages of World War II.

    A. Somua S35

    B. Renault FT

    C. Hotchkiss H35

    D. Toulon B28

92. From which island base did the legendary Cactus Air Force conduct operations?

    A. Guadalcanal

    B. Saipan

    C. Pearl Harbor

    D. Guam

93. These were the only two Italian *Littorio*-class battleships to survive the war.

    A. *Benedetto Brin* and *Lazio*

    B. *Regina Elena* and *Napoli*

    C. *Italia* and *Vittorio Veneto*

    D. *Roma* and *Emanuele Filiberto*

94. Which of the following was the *Yamato's* sister ship?

    A. *Yamashiro*

    B. *Settsu*

    C. *Kawachi*

    D. *Musashi*

95. This Soviet attack aircraft was considered the most effective tank-killer against German armor.

    A. Ilyushin Il-2

    B. Tupolev DB-1

    C. Antonov An-30

    D. Yermolayev Yer-2

96. US Army Air Corps Lieutenants Kenneth Taylor and George Welch collectively shot down six Japanese aircraft during the Pearl Harbor attack. Which single-engine aircraft did they fly?

    A. TBF Stinger

    B. P-32 Intruder

    C. F8F Bearcat

    D. P-40 Warhawk

97. The majority of V-2 rockets were launched at the following cities *except*

    A. London

    B. Moscow

    C. Antwerp

    D. Liege

98. How many crew members operated the Japanese Ha-19 midget submarine?

    A. One

    B. Two

    C. Three

    D. Four

99. Name the country that used anti-tank dogs to disable or destroy enemy armor.

    A. Japan

    B. Soviet Union

    C. Germany

    D. France

100. American historian and author William Manchester called this weapon "an instrument of fear."

    A. P-47 Thunderbolt

    B. F6F Panther

    C. B-17 Flying Fortress

    D. Ju-87 *Stuka*

CHAPTER 4 ANSWERS

1. D. aircraft carrier

2. C. 88 mm

3. C. 385

4. A. Five

5. B. B-24 Liberator

6. B. Carcano Modello 1891

7. A. USS *Pennsylvania*

8. B. Thirteen

9. A. *Admiral Graf Spee*

10. B. "Damn Yankees"

11. C. June 13, 1944

12. B. Liberty ships

13. D. Six

14. A. P-38 Lightning

15. B. Fighter

16. D. the *Yaku*

17. C. M-1 Garand rifle

18. C. the Tempest MK II

19. B. I-58

20. B. tanks

21. B. Eleven

22. B. *Sturmgeschutz* III

23. B. Hawker Aircraft

24. D. the *Daito*

25. D. Two

26. C. Plywood

27. C. Douglas Aircraft

28. A. 8,000 lbs.

29. B. Thirty

30. C. Twenty-four

31. D. Bomb targets in France and Germany

32. A. England

33. C. December 10, 1941

34. B. B-24 Liberator

35. A. No. 4 MK I

36. A. Four

37. B. Nine

38. B. Consolidated Aircraft

39. B. the *Hato*

40. B. Panther

41. C. P-38 Lightning

42. A. HMS *Athenia*

43. D. Non-traversing front turret

44. C. USS *Arizona*

45. C. Willys jeep

46. D. Hudson, Camden, New Jersey

47. C. P-51 Mustang

48. A. USS *Quincy*

49. D. February 1945

50. C. Richard L. Williams

51. D. the USS *Porter*

52. C. 1944

53. D. Mark 14

54. A. flame-throwing tank

55. C. USS *Tripoli*

56. A. Waco CG-4

57. D. the *Tirpitz*

58. C. USS *St. Paul*

59. A. M3 Lee

60. D. All of the above

61. B. Avro Lancaster

62. B. 353

63. A. P-51 Mustang

64. D. 600

65. C. G

66. D. July 30, 1945

67. D. 105 mm

68. C. Single-engine fighter

69. C. B-25 Mitchell

70. B. the Type XXI

71. C. TBF Avenger

72. C. Karabiner 98K

73. B. 360 mph

74. D. USS *Reuben James*

75. B. Two

76. C. P-40 Warhawk

77. C. 50,000

78. A. USS *Juneau*

79. C. Ferdinand

80. D. Grumman Aircraft

81. D. 700

82. B. Four

83. C. United States

84. A. E16A1 seaplane

85. A. Barnes Wallis

86. D. Type 97 Chi-Ra

87. D. M1A1 Thompson

88. B. Twenty-nine

89. C. 80,000

90. A. USS *Gladwyn*

91. B. Renault FT

92. A. Guadalcanal

93. C. *Italia* and *Vittorio Veneto*

94. D. *Musashi*

95. A. Ilyushin II-2

96. D. P-40 Warhawk

97. B. Moscow

98. B. Two

99. B. Soviet Union

100. D. Ju-87 *Stuka*

CHAPTER 5
CODENAMES AND NICKNAMES

1. Which was the codename for the US invasion of New Guinea?

    A. HERO

    B. AUDACIOUS

    C. BROWN

    D. None of the above

2. Known to his men as the "GI General," _____ served as the first chairman of the Joint Chiefs of Staff.

    A. Courtney Hodges

    B. Omar Bradley

    C. Nathan Twining

    D. Jacob Devers

3. Which Japanese admiral was nicknamed "King Kong"?

    A. Takeo Juini

    B. Chuichi Hara

    C. Isoroku Yamamoto

    D. Matsuji Kobe

4. Operation BARBAROSSA was the German plan to invade

    A. Great Britain

    B. the Soviet Union

    C. Norway

    D. Belgium

5. The Allies referred to the Japanese Tachikawa Ki-74 twin-engine bomber as

    A. "Patsy"

    B. "George"

    C. "Hank"

    D. "Ida"

6. All of the following were codenames for the Normandy assault beaches *except*

    A. JUNO

    B. RHINO

    C. OMAHA

    D. SWORD

7. Known as the "Tiger of Malaya," he was executed for war crimes in 1946.

    A. Tadashi Hanaya

    B. Renya Mutaguchi

    C. Tomoyuki Yamashita

    D. Masakazu Kawabe

8. Originally called Operation ANVIL, it was the Allied plan for the invasion of Southern France.

    A. TORNADO

    B. DRAGOON

    C. BOXCAR

    D. OVERLORD

9. Admiral Arleigh Burke's nickname was

    A. "31-Knots"

    B. "Old Rough and Ready"

    C. "Piss and Vinegar"

    D. "Old Ironsides"

10. This Allied airborne operation was the brainchild of Field Marshal Bernard Montgomery.

    A. OCTAGON

    B. JUPITER

    C. ICEBERG

    D. MARKET GARDEN

11. Approximately _____ Japanese warships were sunk during the Battle of Leyte Gulf (Operation SHO-GO).

    A. ten

    B. fifteen

    C. twenty-five

    D. thirty

12. Operation WACHT AM RHEIN was the codename for Germany's

    A. defense of the Ruhr Valley

    B. assault on Moscow

    C. invasion of Sicily

    D. Ardennes offensive

13. Which *South Dakota*-class battleship was nicknamed "Big Mamie?"

    A. USS *Montana*

    B. USS *Alabama*

    C. USS *Massachusetts*

    D. USS *Georgia*

14. The moniker of the US 28th Infantry Division was

    A. "Blue and Gray"

    B. "Dixie"

    C. "The Bloody Bucket"

    D. "Red Bull"

15. Which was the codename for the invasion of Okinawa?

    A. ICEBERG

    B. LONGHORN

    C. BASEBALL

    D. ANGEL

16. The US 30th Infantry Division's nickname was

    A. "Old Reliable"

    B. "Tropic Lightning"

    C. "Old Hickory"

    A. "Red Arrow"

17. "Baldy" was the nickname for which US admiral?

    A. Martin Harrelson

    B. Archibald Howard

    C. Trevor Campbell

    D. Charles Pownall

18. Which weapon was known as "Hitler's Buzzsaw"?

    A. Walther P38

    B. *Maschinengerwehr* 42

    C. *Gewehr* 41

    D. *Sturmgewehr* 44

19. This was the codename for the US seizure of the Gilbert Islands.

    A. BANTAM

    B. GALVANIC

    C. DRUMSTICK

    D. None of the above

20. Which Soviet weapon did German troops refer to as "Stalin's Organ"?

    A. M1931 artillery

    B. T-34 tank

    C. Katyusha rocket launcher

    D. SG-43 machine gun

21. This was the operational name for the US invasion of Guadalcanal.

    A. BEECHNUT

    B. WATCHTOWER

    C. ABERDEEN

    D. CRYSTAL

22. A notorious Nazi guard at Ravensbruck and Auschwitz, she was known as the "Beautiful Beast."

    A. Helga Mueller

    B. Clara Fischer

    C. Irma Grese

    D. Gertrude Wagner

23. How many Japanese soldiers were killed during the Battle of Peleliu (Operation STALEMATE II)?

    A. 6,000

    B. 8,000

    C. 10,000

    D. 15,000

24. The V-1 rocket was known colloquially as the

    A. "Flying Carpet"

    B. "Doodlebug"

    C. "Jim Dandy"

    D. "Hitler Harpoon"

25. Chief of Naval Operations and later commander, US Naval Forces, Europe, _____ received the sobriquet "Betty" as a plebe at Annapolis.

    A. Joseph Fowler

    B. Harold Stark

    C. Raymond Spruance

    D. Walter Anderson

26. Which was the nickname for the German Messerschmitt Me-163?

    A. "Meteor"

    B. "Saturn"

    C. "Komet"

    D. "Jupiter"

27. The United States referred to the Japanese Nakajima Ki-49 heavy bomber as

    A. "Jake"

    B. "Helen"

    C. "Kate"

    D. "Mabel"

28. It was the codename for a British airborne assault on U-boat pens in France.

    A. COUGHDROP

    B. VENDETTA

    C. SEA HORSE

    D. RODEO

29. The "Black Dragon" was the nickname for which decorated battleship?

    A. USS *New Jersey*

    B. USS *Wisconsin*

    C. USS *Missouri*

    D. USS *Iowa*

30. Operation CATECHISM was the RAF mission to destroy the

    A. *Bismarck*

    B. *Prince Eugen*

    C. *Tirpitz*

    D. *Scharnhorst*

31. The Japanese Nakajima Ki-43 single-engine fighter was more commonly known as

    A. "Felix"

    B. "Dave"

    C. "Edna"

    D. "Oscar"

32. *Panzerknacker* was the German word for the

    A. Tupolev assault rifle

    B. Dreyse rocket launcher

    C. Purplenko medium bomber

    D. *Hafthohlladung* anti-tank device

33. The Allies referred to the Japanese Kawasaki Ki-61 fighter as

    A. "Tony"

    B. "Adam"

    C. "Baka"

    D. "Cherry"

34. Which of the following military units was known as the "Steamroller?"

    A. British 9th Infantry Division

    B. US 3rd Cavalry Division

    C. Polish 78th Infantry Division

    D. None of the above

35. This was the codename for the atomic bomb dropped on Nagasaki.

    A. "Fat Man"

    B. "Simple Simon"

    C. "Little Boy"

    D. "Slim Jim"

36. "Ronson" and "Rhino" were nicknames for which of the following tanks?

    A. M24 Chaffee

    B. Roubaix R56

    C. M4 Sherman

    D. Matilda II

37. Known as "Big Ben," this *Essex*-class aircraft carrier was heavily damaged by Japanese bombs late in the war but survived and was decommissioned in 1947.

    A. USS *Bunker Hill*

    B. USS *Intrepid*

    C. USS *Belleau Woods*

    D. USS *Franklin*

38. The buildup of Allied forces for the invasion of Nazi-occupied France was codenamed

    A. PINCER

    B. CHARIOT

    C. JERICHO

    D. BOLERO

39. Which was the codename for the atomic bomb dropped on Hiroshima?

    A. "Fertile Myrtle"

    B. "Little Boy"

    C. "Fat Man"

    D. "Calamity Jane"

40. Operation FORTITUDE was the Allied deception plan prior to the invasion of

    A. Okinawa

    B. Normandy

    C. Sicily

    D. Iwo Jima

41. A-GO was the codename for the Japanese plan to

    A. destroy US naval forces off Saipan

    B. recapture Guadalcanal

    C. invade the Western United States

    D. block the US invasion of Honshu

42. This German tank commander was known as the "Black Baron."

    A. Kurt Knispel

    B. Michael Wittman

    C. Otto Jurgen

    D. Peter Schmidt

43. Which US general was nicknamed "Old Gravel Voice"?

    A. Ernest Harmon

    B. Leland Hobbs

    C. John Matthews

    D. Orlando Ward

44. _____ were movable iron fences used by the Germans as anti-tank obstacles.

    A. "Grim Reapers"

    B. "Jodl's Brass Bombers"

    C. "Belgian Gates"

    D. "Hitler's Grasshoppers"

45. "Bull" was the nickname for which US admiral?

    A.   William Davis

    B.   Joseph Reeves

    C.   Christopher Wilson

    D.   James Henderson

46. The moniker of the British 7th Armoured Division was

    A.   "Tommies"

    B.   "The Desert Rats"

    C.   "Queen's Best"

    D.   "The Pythons"

47. Operation VENGEANCE was the United States plan to kill

    A.   Hideki Tojo

    B.   Erwin Rommel

    C.   Isoroku Yamamoto

    D.   Heinrich Himmler

48. Which weapon was nicknamed the "Walking *Stuka*"?

    A.   *Wurfrahmen* 40

    B.   *Steyr* M1913

    C.   *Kampfmesser* 42

    D.   *Seitengewehr* 98

49. This was the codename for the planned invasion of Japan.

    A. Operation COMPOSITION

    B. Operation DOWNFALL

    C. Operation SAPPHIRE

    D. None of the above

50. He was known to Allied forces as "Smiling Albert."

    A. Albert Wedemeyer

    B. Albert von Becker

    C. Albert Kenner

    D. Albert Kesselring

51. Which US officer was known as "Skinny"?

    A. Jonathan Wainwright

    B. Walter Craig

    C. James Edward Moore

    D. George P. Hays

52. The US 2nd Armored Division's nickname was

    A. "Old Ironsides"

    B. "Spearhead"

    C. "Breakthrough"

    D. "Hell on Wheels"

53. Which was the official designation for the Japanese Val?

    A. Nakajima C6N

    B. Kawasaki Ki-18

    C. Mitsubishi F1M

    D. Aichi D3A2

54. Devised by General Omar Bradley, _____ led to the breakout of Allied forces in Normandy.

    A. Operation CORKSCREW

    B. Operation STONEWALL

    C. Operation COBRA

    D. Operation HARPOON

55. The codename for the US assault on the Mariana Islands was

    A. CACTUS

    B. TRUMPET

    C. AJAX

    D. FORAGER

56. "Fork-Tailed Devil" was the German nickname for the

    A. F4D Skyray

    B. P-38 Lightning

    C. P-51 Mustang

    D. C-47 Dakota

57. This was the codename for the initial detonation of the atomic bomb on July 16, 1945.

    A. POLARIS

    B. TRINITY

    C. ATLAS

    D. TRIDENT

58. General Matthew Ridgway was affectionately known as

    A. "Old Blood and Guts"

    B. "Big Ridge"

    C. "Old Iron Tits"

    D. "The Old Man"

59. Which was the infamous name given to the US M3 half-track?

    A. "Widow Maker"

    B. "Purple Heart Box"

    C. "Death Ride"

    D. "Coffin Carrier"

60. An SS doctor who conducted sadistic experiments at Auschwitz, he was known as the "Angel of Death."

    A. Josef Mengele

    B. Sepp Gruber

    C. Erich Bauer

    D. Hermann Becker

61. This British air and sea operation called for the capture of Rangoon.

    A. DRACULA

    B. FRANKENSTEIN

    C. PINPOINT

    D. DAGGER

62. "Emil" was the common moniker for the

    A. Dornier Do 217

    B. Macchi C205

    C. Messerschmitt Bf 109E

    D. Caproni Vizzola F6

63. The more familiar name for the US Piper L-4 reconnaissance plane was the

    A. "Grasshopper"

    B. "Kangaroo"

    C. "Pigeon"

    D. "Butterfly"

64. American-born actress who became a Nazi propagandist, she was dubbed "Axis Sally" by American troops. Her real name was

    A. Betty Constantine

    B. Marjorie Powers

    C. Donna Krauss

    D. Mildred Gillars

65. Nicknamed the "Gargoyle," he was an admiral in the Imperial Japanese Navy and the last serving commander-in-chief of the Combined Fleet.

    A. Kiyoshi Imai

    B. Jisaburo Ozawa

    C. Nobuyushi Muto

    D. Okitsugi Arao

66. Initially called Operation GYMNAST, Operation TORCH was the Allied plan for the

    A. invasion of North Africa

    B. airborne drop on Berlin

    C. blockade of Tokyo Harbor

    D. None of the above

67. The TBF Avenger was known as the

    A. "Blue Buffalo"

    B. "Scorpion"

    C. "Pregnant Beast"

    D. "Black Bird"

68. "Seagull" was the nickname for which Soviet fighter?

    A. Mikoyan K-29

    B. Polikarpov I-153

    C. Antonov An-140

    D. Sukhoi Su-27

69. The commander-in-chief of the US Battle Fleet and later president of the US Naval War College, his nickname was "Old Dutch."

    A. Walter Cowles

    B. Cameron Winslow

    C. Edward Kalbfus

    D. Thomas Howard

70. Operation _____ was the codename for the invasion of the Italian mainland by the US 5th Army.

    A. WORKHORSE

    B. CARPENTER

    C. WALLOP

    D. AVALANCHE

71. Proposed by General Douglas MacArthur, this operation called for the capture of Rabaul.

    A. VELVET

    B. FATIGUE

    C. WHIPSAW

    D. ELKTON

72. The nickname for the Martin B-26 medium bomber was

    A. "Widow Maker"

    B. "Little Shaver"

    C. "Peter Pan"

    D. "Big Deal"

73. _____ was the more common name for the Japanese Mitsubishi F1M2 observation seaplane.

    A. "Billy"

    B. "Denise"

    C. "Simon"

    D. "Pete"

74. "Black Devils" was the moniker for which military unit?

    A. British 4th Infantry Division

    B. 1st Special Service Force

    C. US 79th Airborne Division

    D. Canadian 8th Commando Brigade

75. Which was the nickname of the Japanese Mitsubishi Ki-57 transport plane?

    A. "Rita"

    B. "Jenny"

    C. "Topsy"

    D. "Charlie"

76. Operation ATILLA was the codename for the

    A. US occupation of postwar Berlin

    B. British seizure of Italian naval bases in the Mediterranean

    C. German occupation of Vichy France

    D. Allied advance in Burma

77. Known as "the Spearhead," they took part in the Battle of Iwo Jima.

    A. US 1st Marine Division

    B. US 2nd Marine Division

    C. US 5th Marine Division

    D. US 6th Marine Division

78. The nickname for the US 13th Armored Division was the

    A. "Black Cats"

    B. "Thundering Herd"

    C. "Phantoms"

    D. "Liberators"

79. Which was the nickname of the Japanese American woman who made propaganda broadcasts for Japan?

    A. "Tokyo Rose"

    B. "Olive Oil"

    C. "Tiger Lily"

    D. "Honshu Hannah"

80. The US 17th Airborne Division's nickname was

    A. "Golden Talons"

    B. "Texas"

    C. "Rock of the Marne"

    D. "Santa Fe"

81. It was the Allied name for the Japanese Kawanishi E7K floatplane.

    A. "Boris"

    B. "Caroline"

    C. "Natasha"

    D. "Alf"

82. Which was the Allied nickname for the German stick grenade?

    A. "Banana Peel"

    B. "Firecracker"

    C. "Potato Masher"

    D. "Carrot Stick"

83. This operation was the Japanese plan to defend the homeland from an Allied invasion.

    A. SOKONAU

    B. KETSU-GO

    C. HINODE

    D. NIKKOU

84. Which was the German nickname for the British 43rd Infantry Division?

    A. "Blue Demons"

    B. "Red Devils"

    C. "Black Knights"

    D. "Yellow Devils"

85. Known as "Black Jack," he was the tactical commander of US naval forces at the Battle of the Coral Sea.

    A. Frank Fletcher

    B. John McCain

    C. George Mitchell

    D. John Stevens

86. The depraved wife of a concentration camp commandant, she was called the "Bitch of Buchenwald."

    A. Else Holstein

    B. Ilse Koch

    C. Gisela Miete

    D. Alberta Reinefarth

87. Which weapon did US troops nickname the "Screaming Mimi"?

    A. *Gewehr* 43

    B. *Sauer* 38H

    C. *Nebelwerfer* 41

    D. *Lugar* Po 8

88. The German plan to invade Denmark and Norway was designated Operation

    A. WESERUBUNG

    B. OST

    C. BODDEN

    D. URSULA

89. He was known to his fellow British officers as "Sunshine."

    A.   Dudley St. John

    B.   John Crocker

    C.   Kenneth Anderson

    D.   None of the above

90. William Joyce was an Irish American citizen who became a propaganda broadcaster for Nazi Germany. His radio name was

    A.   "Prince Adolf"

    B.   "Field Marshal Fritz"

    C.   "Lord Haw-Haw"

    D.   "Colonel Kraut"

91. An officer in the Imperial Japanese Army who was dubbed "Lawrence of Manchuria," he was tried for war crimes and executed in 1948.

    A.   Sadao Araki

    B.   Ando Teibi

    C.   Isamu Cho

    D.   Kenji Doihara

92. The operational name for German attacks on Allied shipping in the North Atlantic was

    A.   TANNENBERG

    B.   NORDMARK

    C.   HABICHT

    D.   BERNHARD

93. Known as "the Old Breed," they saw action on Guadalcanal and Okinawa.

    A.   US 1st Marine Division

    B.   US 3rd Marine Division

    C.   US 5th Marine Division

    D.   US 7th Marine Division

94. Which was the nickname of the Luftwaffe's Dornier Do 17?

    A.   "Flying Turnip"

    B.   "Flying Cigar"

    C.   "Flying Pencil"

    D.   "Flying Sausage"

95. The Japanese Nakajima B5N2 carrier-borne torpedo bomber was more commonly known as

    A.   "Oak"

    B.   "Kate"

    C.   "Walnut"

    D.   "Jenny"

96. It was an ambitious British operation to drop mines in the English Channel.

    A.   BUTTERMILK

    B.   SEA BISCUIT

    C.   BUCKWHEAT

    D.   GERONIMO

97. Operation _____ was the codename for the Japanese invasion of the Philippines.

    A. B

    B. D

    C. G

    D. M

98. "Mulberry" was the name given to the artificial harbor created for the invasion of

    A. Dieppe

    B. Guadalcanal

    C. Borneo

    D. Normandy

99. The US 2nd Marine Division saw combat on Tarawa and Okinawa. They were proudly called

    A. "Double Trouble"

    B. "Deuces High"

    C. "The Silent Second"

    D. "Two's Company"

100. Who was known to his fellow British officers as "Jumbo"?

    A. Desmond Anderson

    B. Henry Wilson

    C. John Dill

    D. Daniel Beak

CHAPTER 5 ANSWERS

1. D. None of the above

2. B. Omar Bradley

3. B. Chuichi Hara

4. B. the Soviet Union

5. A. "Patsy"

6. B. RHINO

7. C. Tomoyuki Yamashita

8. B. DRAGOON

9. A. "31-Knots"

10. D. MARKET GARDEN

11. C. twenty-five

12. D. Ardennes offensive

13. C. USS *Massachusetts*

14. C. "The Bloody Bucket"

15. A. ICEBERG

16. C. "Old Hickory"

17. D. Charles Pownall

18. B. *Maschinengewehr* 42

19. B. GALVANIC

20. C. Katyusha rocket launcher

21. B. WATCHTOWER

22. C. Irma Grese

23. C. 10,000

24. B. "Doodlebug"

25. B. Harold Stark

26. C. "Komet"

27. B. "Helen"

28. A. COUGHDROP

29. A. USS *New Jersey*

30. C. *Tirpitz*

31. D. "Oscar"

32. D. *Hafthohlladung* anti-tank device

33. A. "Tony"

34. D. None of the above

35. A. "Fat Man"

36. C. M4 Sherman

37. D. USS *Franklin*

38. D. BOLERO

39. B. "Little Boy"

40. B. Normandy

41. A. destroy US naval forces off Saipan

42. B. Michael Wittman

43. A. Ernest Harmon

44. C. "Belgian Gates"

45. B. Joseph Reeves

46. B. "The Desert Rats"

47. C. Isoroku Yamamoto

48. A. *Wurfrahmen* 40

49. B. Operation DOWNFALL

50. D. Albert Kesselring

51. A. Jonathan Wainwright

52. D. "Hell on Wheels"

53. D. Aichi D3A2

54. C. Operation COBRA

55. D. FORAGER

56. B. P-38 Lightning

57. B. TRINITY

58. C. "Old Iron Tits"

59. B. "Purple Heart Box"

60. A. Josef Mengele

61. A. DRACULA

62. C. Messerschmitt Bf 109E

63. A. "Grasshopper"

64. D. Mildred Gillars

65. B. Jisaburo Ozawa

66. A. invasion of North Africa

67. C. "Pregnant Beast"

68. B. Polikarpov I-153

69. C. Edward Kalbfus

70. D. AVALANCHE

71. D. ELKTON

72. A. "Widow Maker"

73. D. "Pete"

74. C. 1st Special Service Force

75. C. "Topsy"

76. C. German occupation of Vichy France

77. C. US 5th Marine Division

78. A. "Black Cats"

79. A. "Tokyo Rose"

80. A. "Golden Talons"

81. D. "Alf"

82. C. "Potato Masher"

83. B. KETSU-GO

84. D. "Yellow Devils"

85. A. Frank Fletcher

86. B. Ilse Koch

87. C. *Nebelwerfer* 41

88. A. WESERUBUNG

89. C. Kenneth Anderson

90. C. "Lord Haw-Haw"

91. D. Kenji Doihara

92. B. NORDMARK

93. A. US 1st Marine Division

94. C. "Flying Pencil"

95. B. "Kate"

96. A. BUTTERMILK

97. D. M

98. D. Normandy

99. C. "The Silent Second"

100. B. Henry Wilson

CHAPTER 6
WARTIME QUOTES

1. "Almighty God: Our sons, pride of our Nation, this day have set upon a mighty endeavor, a struggle to preserve our Republic, our religion, and our civilization, and to set free a suffering humanity."

   A. President Harry Truman

   B. Secretary of War Henry Stimson

   C. President Franklin Roosevelt

   D. Secretary of State Cordell Hull

2. "May God have mercy on my enemies, because I won't."

   A. General George Patton

   B. *Obersturmbannfuhrer* Joachim Peiper

   C. General Tomoyuki Yamashita

   D. General Hasso von Manteuffel

3. "They fought together as brothers-in-arms. They died together and now they lay side by side. To them we have a solemn obligation."

   A. Admiral Harold Stark

   B. General Julian Smith

   C. Admiral Chester Nimitz

   D. General Webb Barrett

4. "The raising of that flag on Suribachi means a Marine Corps for the next 500 years."

   A. General Holland Smith

   B. Secretary of War Henry Stimson

   C. General Roy Geiger

   D. Secretary of the Navy James Forrestal

5. "We and our allies owe and acknowledge an ever-lasting debt of gratitude to the armies and people of the Soviet Union."

    A.   Secretary of State Cordell Hull

    B.   General George Marshall

    C.   Secretary of the Navy Frank Knox

    D.   Vice President Henry Wallace

6. "In the burning and devastated cities, we daily experienced the direct impact of war. It spurred us to do our utmost."

    A.   Hermann Goering

    B.   Albert Speer

    C.   Joseph Goebbels

    D.   Heinrich Himmler

7. "Attacks on cities are strategically justified in so far as they tend to shorten the war and so preserve the lives of Allied soldiers."

    A.   Air Marshal Arthur Harris

    B.   General Richard Sutherland

    C.   Field Marshal John Dill

    D.   General Henry Arnold

8. "That road to V-E Day was hard and long and traveled by weary and valiant men. And history will always record where that road began. It began here, with the first foot prints on the beaches of Normandy."

    A.   President John F. Kennedy

    B.   Senator John McCain

    C.   President George W. Bush

    D.   Senator Lindsey Graham

9. "These are the boys of Pointe du Hoc. These are the men who took the cliffs. These are the champions who helped free a continent."

    A.   President George H.W. Bush

    B.   General Maxwell Taylor

    C.   Senator Barry Goldwater

    D.   President Ronald Reagan

10. "The reason that the American Navy does so well in wartime, is that war is chaos, and the Americans practice chaos on a daily basis."

    A.   Admiral Kurt-Caesar Hoffman

    B.   Admiral Theodor Krancke

    C.   Admiral Helmuth Brinkmann

    D.   Admiral Karl Doenitz

11. "Gentlemen, we are being killed on the beaches. Let us go inland and be killed."

    A.   General Charles Gerhardt

    B.   General William Knudsen

    C.   General Norman Cota

    D.   General Stanley Embick

12. "I'll never forgive the Army for not taking at least part of the blame for Pearl Harbor. That was why I didn't like Stimson."

    A.   Admiral Wilson Brown

    B.   Admiral Ernest King

    C.   Admiral Herbert Leary

    D.   Admiral Thomas Hart

13. "There are no reluctant leaders. A real leader must really want the job."

    A.   General Ira Eaker

    B.   General Thomas Scott

    C.   General Peter Bridges

    D.   None of the above

14. "In our victory over Japan, air power was unquestionably decisive."

    A.   General Joseph McNarney

    B.   General Carl Spaatz

    C.   General George Brett

    D.   General Curtis LeMay

15. "If we should have to fight, we should be prepared to do so from the neck up instead of from the neck down."

    A.   General Jimmy Doolittle

    B.   Admiral William Miller

    C.   General Robert North

    D.   Admiral William Halsey

16. "The best political weapon is the weapon of terror. Cruelty commands respect."

    A.   Rudolf Hess

    B.   Heinrich Himmler

    C.   Julius Streicher

    D.   Alfred Rosenberg

17. "Air superiority is a condition for all operations, at sea, in land, and in the air."

    A.   Air Marshal Arthur Tedder

    B.   Field Marshal Bernard Montgomery

    C.   Admiral Andrew Cunningham

    D.   General Kenneth Delos

18. "We're at war with Japan. We were attacked by Japan. Do you want to kill Japanese, or would you rather have Americans killed?"

    A.   Speaker of the House Sam Rayburn

    B.   General Frank Merrill

    C.   President Franklin Roosevelt

    D.   General Curtis LeMay

19. "The smell of death overwhelmed us even before we passed through the stockade. More than 3,200 naked, emaciated bodies have been flung into shallow graves."

    A.   General Omar Bradley

    B.   General William Morris

    C.   General Carlos Brewer

    D.   General Louis Hibbs

20. "It is my opinion that the use of this barbarous weapon at Hiroshima and Nagasaki was of no material assistance in our war against Japan."

    A.   General Douglas MacArthur

    B.   Secretary of State James Byrnes

    C.   Admiral William Leahy

    D.   General Leslie Groves

21. "Gentlemen, you are about to witness the most famous victory in history."

    A.   Field Marshal William Slim

    B.   Air Marshal Arthur Tedder

    C.   Prime Minister Winston Churchill

    D.   Adolf Hitler

22. "Before we're through with them, the Japanese language will be spoken only in Hell!"

    A.   General Walter Krueger

    B.   Admiral William Halsey

    C.   General George Patton

    D.   Admiral Ernest King

23. "We are not retreating; we are advancing in another direction."

    A.   Admiral Husband E. Kimmel

    B.   General George Kenney

    C.   President Franklin Roosevelt

    D.   None of the above

24. "The Japanese position was hopeless even before the first atomic bomb fell because the Japanese had lost control of their own air."

    A.   Admiral Frank Fletcher

    B.   General Charles Summerall

    C.   Admiral Albert Zimmerman

    D.   General Henry Arnold

25. "The first twenty-four hours of the invasion will be decisive.... For the Allies, as well as Germany, it will be the longest day."

    A.   General Wilhelm Adam

    B.   Field Marshal Erwin Rommel

    C.   General Franz Halder

    D.   Field Marshal Gerd von Rundstedt

26. "A bright light filled the plane. The first shock waves hit us. We were eleven and a half miles slant average from the atomic explosion but the whole airplane cracked and crinkled from the blast."

    A.   Colonel Paul Tibbets

    B.   Lieutenant Caleb Mitchell

    C.   Major Richard Bong

    D.   Captain Andrew Burke

27. "Your task will not be an easy one. Your enemy is well-trained, well-equipped, and battle-hardened. He will fight savagely."

    A.   General George Marshall

    B.   Colonel Chesty Puller

    C.   General Dwight Eisenhower

    D.   Admiral Harry Yarnell

28. "The Anglo-Saxons have set foot on our soil. France is becoming a battlefield."

    A.   General Philippe Petain

    B.   General Maurice Gamelin

    C.   General Charles de Gaulle

    D.   General Henri Giraud

29. "They sowed the wind, and now they are going to reap the whirlwind."

    A.   General Hideki Tojo

    B.   Air Marshal Arthur Harris

    C.   General Brehon Somervell

    D.   Air Marshal Charles Burnett

30. "As a result of the cold, the machine guns were no longer able to fire.... The result of all this was a panic."

    A.   Field Marshal Erwin Rommel

    B.   General Omar Bradley

    C.   Field Marshal Walter Mueller

    D.   General Heinz Guderian

31. "A man can scarcely pride himself on having smitten a sleeping enemy; it is more a matter of shame, simply, for the one smitten."

    A.   Field Marshal Wilhelm Keitel

    B.   Benito Mussolini

    C.   Admiral Isoroku Yamamoto

    D.   Adolf Hitler

32. "Why piddle about making porridge with artillery, and then send men to drown themselves in it for a hundred yards of NO MAN'S LAND? Tanks mean advances of miles at a time not yards!"

    A.   Captain Basil Liddell-Hart

    B.   General Percy Hobart

    C.   Prime Minister Winston Churchill

    D.   General Neil Ritchie

33. "Humility must always be the portion of any man who receives acclaim earned in blood of his followers and sacrifices of his friends."

    A. Admiral Chester Nimitz

    B. Field Marshal Harold Alexander

    C. Lord Louis Mountbatten

    D. General Dwight Eisenhower

34. "Two kinds of people are staying on this beach: the dead and those who are going to die."

    A. Colonel George Taylor

    B. General Theodore Roosevelt Jr.

    C. Major Bernard Wilson

    D. General Raymond Barton

35. "Well, is it or isn't it the invasion?"

    A. Field Marshal Gerd von Rundstedt

    B. General Hans Speidel

    C. Adolf Hitler

    D. None of the above

36. "We shall see who fights better and who dies more easily."

    A. General Alfred Jodl

    B. Field Marshal Albert Kesselring

    C. General Johannes Blasko

    D. Field Marshal Walter Model

37. "If anyone has any doubts in his mind, let him stay behind."

    A.   Field Marshal Bernard Montgomery

    B.   General Dwight Eisenhower

    C.   Prime Minister Winston Churchill

    D.   General Karl Mueller

38. "Win the air war and isolate the battlefield."

    A.   General Carl Spaatz

    B.   General Ira Eaker

    C.   General Jimmy Doolittle

    D.   General Nathan Twining

39. "I've had my fill of Hitler. These conferences called by the ringing of a bell are not to my liking; the bell is rung when people call their servants."

    A.   Prime Minister Edouard Daladier

    B.   General Francisco Franco

    C.   Prime Minister Neville Chamberlain

    D.   Benito Mussolini

40. "The fruits of victory are tumbling into our mouths too quickly."

    A.   Fumimaro Konoe

    B.   Mitsumasa Yonai

    C.   Emperor Hirohito

    D.   Kichisaburo Nomura

41. "We knew the world would not be the same. A few people laughed, a few people cried, most people were silent."

    A.   Hans Bethe

    B.   J. Robert Oppenheimer

    C.   Albert Einstein

    D.   Ernest O. Lawrence

42. "I claim we got a hell of a beating. We got run out of Burma, and it is as humiliating as hell."

    A.   Air Marshal Leonard Slatter

    B.   Lord Louis Mountbatten

    C.   Field Marshal Jan Smuts

    D.   General Joseph Stilwell

43. "Under proper guidance, in the course of the Final Solution, the Jews are to be allocated for appropriate labor in the East."

    A.   Reinhard Heydrich

    B.   Adolf Hitler

    C.   Josef Mengele

    D.   Adolf Eichmann

44. "The war against Russia is an important chapter in the German nation's struggle for existence."

    A.   Field Marshal Gunther von Kluge

    B.   General Kurt Student

    C.   Field Marshal Georg von Kuchler

    D.   General Franz Halder

45. "Our cause is just. The enemy will be defeated. Victory is ours."

    A.   Foreign Minister Vyacheslav Molotov

    B.   General Harry Crerar

    C.   Prime Minister Winston Churchill

    D.   Field Marshal Robert Ritter von Greim

46. "Nothing chastens a planner more than the knowledge that he will have to carry out the plan."

    A.   Field Marshal Erich von Manstein

    B.   Admiral James Richardson

    C.   General James Gavin

    D.   Field Marshal Wolfram Freiherr von Richthofen

47. "Above all, we shall dedicate ourselves and our entire strength to the defense of the island. Each man will make it his duty to kill ten of the enemy before dying."

    A.   General Tadamichi Kuribayashi

    B.   Admiral Keiji Shibazaki

    C.   General Mitsuru Ushuri

    D.   Admiral Kunio Nakagawa

48. "We must be very careful not to assign to this deliverance the attribute of a victory. Wars are not won by evacuations."

    A.   General Maxime Weygand

    B.   Prime Minister Edouard Daladier

    C.   General Alan Cunningham

    D.   Prime Minister Winston Churchill

49. "As a soldier he is a bad politician, and as a politician is an equally bad soldier."

    A. Justice Felix Frankfurter

    B. President Harry Truman

    C. Field Marshal Bernard Montgomery

    D. None of the above

50. "We are now in this war. We are all in it, all the way."

    A. Prime Minister Winston Churchill

    B. President Franklin Roosevelt

    C. Prime Minister Neville Chamberlain

    D. Foreign Secretary Anthony Eden

51. "Sure, we want to go home. We want this war over with."

    A. General George Patton

    B. General Norman Kirk

    C. General William Sheep

    D. General Clarence McCarney

52. "I'll come back as soon as I can with as much as I can."

    A. General James Magee

    B. Admiral William Halsey

    C. Field Marshal Erwin Rommel

    D. General Douglas MacArthur

53. "Books cannot be killed. People die, but books never die."

    A.   President Franklin Roosevelt

    B.   Dietrich Bonhoeffer

    C.   Adolf Hitler

    D.   Martin von Mueller

54. "The Chinese soldier was tough, brave, and experienced. After all he had been fighting on his own without help for years."

    A.   Air Marshal Ralph Cochrane

    B.   General Clarence Bird

    C.   Field Marshal William Slim

    D.   General Lionel Cox

55. "In a life and death struggle, we cannot afford to leave our destinies in the hands of failures."

    A.   Prime Minister Clement Attlee

    B.   Ambassador Joseph P. Kennedy

    C.   Governor Thomas Dewey

    D.   Attorney General Francis Biddle

56. "Before Alamein, we had no victories. After Alamein, we had no defeats."

    A.   General Desmond Anderson

    B.   Prime Minister Winston Churchill

    C.   General Roy Urquhart

    D.   Field Marshal Bernard Montgomery

57. "Mussolini is quite humiliated because our troops have not moved a step forward."

    A. General Alfredo Guzzoni

    B. Field Marshal Pietro Badoglio

    C. Foreign Minister Galeazzo Ciano

    D. Field Marshal Giovanni Messe

58. "It had been a frontal assault in broad daylight, against a mined beach defended by all the obstacles military ingenuity could devise."

    A. Charles Collingswood

    B. John Daly

    C. Ernest Hemingway

    D. Eric Sevareid

59. "To every man of us, Tobruk was a symbol of British resistance, and we were now going to finish with it for good."

    A. Field Marshal Erwin Rommel

    B. General Leslie Morshead

    C. Field Marshal Hermann von Eichhorn

    D. General Ronald Scobie

60. "Soldiers were and will remain soldiers. They fight, not thinking about the reasons, true to their military oath."

    A. General Hans-Jurgen von Arnim

    B. Field Marshal Friedrich Paulus

    C. General Gusztav Jany

    D. Field Marshal Karl von Bulow

61. "Like so many of our people, we have had a personal experience of German barbarity which strengthens the resolution of all of us to fight through to final victory."

    A. King George VI

    B. Field Marshal Harold Alexander

    C. King Edward VIII

    D. General James Weber Smith

62. "In my opinion, the limit of endurance has been reached by the troops under my command."

    A. General Field Harris

    B. Field Marshal Walter von Stronheim

    C. General Bernard Freyberg

    D. Admiral Thomas St. James

63. "We did not intend to fight enemy warships.... The crew have behaved magnificently. We shall win or die."

    A. Captain Hans Langsdorff

    B. Admiral Gunther Lutjens

    C. Captain Joachim Mueller

    D. Admiral Erich Raeder

64. "A gigantic fleet has amassed in Pearl Harbor. This fleet will be utterly crushed with one blow at the very beginning of hostilities."

    A. Admiral Chuichi Nagumo

    B. Admiral Husband E. Kimmel

    C. Admiral Seiichi Ito

    D. Admiral William Pye

65. "I say that the bombing of the abbey was a mistake. It only made our job more difficult, more costly in terms of men, machines, and time."

    A.   General Wolfgang Brandenstein

    B.   General Mark Clark

    C.   General Heinrich von Vietinghoff

    D.   General Oliver Leese

66. "The enemy knows that he must wipe out our fighters. Once he has done that, he will be able to play football with the German people."

    A.   General Ernst Buffa

    B.   Field Marshal Hugo Sperrle

    C.   General Werner Anton

    D.   Field Marshal Erhard Milch

67. "We have just received your reply. The Japanese Army will consider nothing but surrender."

    A.   General Kuniaki Koiso

    B.   Field Marshal Kotohito Kanin

    C.   General Tomoyuki Yamashita

    D.   Field Marshal Hajime Sugiyama

68. "I should like to pay the highest tribute for the most gallant fight put up against impossible odds."

    A.   Air Marshal Leslie Gossage

    B.   Foreign Secretary Anthony Eden

    C.   Prime Minister Winston Churchill

    D.   Admiral John Tovey

69. "I have full confidence in your courage, devotion to duty, and skill in battle. We will accept nothing less than full victory!"

    A. General George Patton

    B. President Franklin Roosevelt

    C. General Dwight Eisenhower

    D. President Harry Truman

70. "Today we rule Germany, tomorrow the world."

    A. Max Steiner

    B. Joseph Goebbels

    C. Adolf Hitler

    D. Hermann Goering

71. "They [women Marines] don't have a nickname, and they don't need one.... They are Marines."

    A. General William Brice

    B. Admiral Dudley Brown

    C. General Clifton Cates

    D. None of the above

72. "This is a fight between a free world and a slave world."

    A. Secretary of Labor Frances Perkins

    B. Vice President Henry Wallace

    C. Secretary of the Interior Harold Ickes

    D. Assistant Secretary of State Dean Acheson

73. "A thousand years will pass, and the guilt of Germany will not be erased."

    A.   Hans Frank

    B.   Karl Korner

    C.   Anne Frank

    D.   Heinz Keppler

74. "If and when the war starts, no matter where or whoever you are or if you are young or old, Northerner or Southerner, you all have the responsibility of protecting our home and repelling the enemy."

    A.   Chiang Kai-shek

    B.   Ho Chi Minh

    C.   Adolf Hitler

    D.   Josip Tito

75. "The gallantry and aggressive fighting spirit of the Russian soldiers command the American Army's admiration."

    A.   General Terry Allen

    B.   General George Marshall

    C.   General Walter Brooks

    D.   General John Miller

76. "I'll tell you what bravery really is. Bravery is just determination to do a job that you know has to be done."

    A.   Captain Thomas McGuire

    B.   Major Francis Gabreski

    C.   Captain Joe Foss

    D.   Lieutenant Audie Murphy

77. "I look upon the Guadalcanal and Tulagi operations as the turning point from offensive to defensive, and the cause of our setback there was our inability to increase our forces at the same speed as you."

    A. Admiral Chuichi Nagumo

    B. General Hitoshi Imamura

    C. Admiral Osami Nagano

    D. General Harukichi Hyakutake

78. "I wish you to dispel by all possible means the idea that Rommel represents something more than an ordinary general."

    A. Air Marshal John Slessor

    B. Field Marshal Claude Auchinleck

    C. Air Marshal J. D. Breakey

    D. Field Marshal John Vereker

79. "There is a denial of the value of the individual. Christianity affirms the value of each individual soul. Nazism denies it."

    A. Prime Minister Winston Churchill

    B. President Franklin Roosevelt

    C. Prime Minister Clement Attlee

    D. General Charles de Gaulle

80. "Bataan is like a child in a family who dies. It lives in our hearts."

    A. General Jonathan Wainwright

    B. President Franklin Roosevelt

    C. General Douglas MacArthur

    D. Admiral John Towers

81. "No soldier ever really survives a war."

    A. Major Richard Bong

    B. Commander David Campbell

    C. Lieutenant Audie Murphy

    D. Major Lofton Henderson

82. "No one person invented Mulberry. The knowledge that we had to have this floating harbor slowly grew."

    A. General Dwight Eisenhower

    B. Lord Louis Mountbatten

    C. Field Marshal Bernard Montgomery

    D. Admiral Henry Hewitt

83. "Once Japan is destroyed as an aggressive force, we know of no other challenging power that can appear in the Pacific."

    A. Admiral Husband E. Kimmel

    B. General Walter Short

    C. Admiral James Richardson

    D. Ambassador Joseph Grew

84. "It is evil things that we will be fighting against: brute force, bad faith, injustice, oppression, and persecution, and against them I am certain that the right will prevail."

    A. President Wladyslaw Raczkiewicz

    B. Prime Minister Edouard Daladier

    C. President Harry Truman

    D. Prime Minister Neville Chamberlain

85. "Should hostilities once break out between Japan and the United States, it is not enough that we take Guam and the Philippines, nor even Hawaii and San Francisco. To make victory certain, we would march into Washington and dictate the terms of peace in the White House."

    A.   Admiral Hiroaki Abe

    B.   General Takeo Kondo

    C.   Admiral Isoroku Yamamoto

    D.   General Tadamichi Kuribayashi

86. "If I live, I will fight, wherever I must, as long as I must, until the enemy is defeated, and the national stain washed clean."

    A.   Admiral Jean Darlan

    B.   General Henri Giraud

    C.   Admiral Philippe Auboyneau

    D.   General Charles de Gaulle

87. "I walked by the crowds of civilians, within three or four feet of them, in rags and half starved, and never once did I have any occasion to fear them."

    A.   Lieutenant Robert Hanson

    B.   Colonel Pappy Boyington

    C.   Captain Joe Foss

    D.   Major George Preddy

88. "I have done what any red-blooded American would do. We gonna do our part, and we will win, because we are on God's side."

    A. Joe Louis

    B. Ted Williams

    C. Joe DiMaggio

    D. Yogi Berra

89. "There is no choice but to force a decisive fleet encounter. If we set out from here to do that and we go to the bottom of the Pacific ... things will be peaceful on the high seas for some time."

    A. Admiral Chuichi Nagumo

    B. General Hideki Tojo

    C. Commander Mitsuo Fuchida

    D. Admiral Isoroku Yamamoto

90. "Look at an infantryman's eyes, and you can tell how much war he has seen."

    A. Ernie Pyle

    B. Bill Mauldin

    C. Ernest Hemingway

    D. Edward R. Murrow

91. "Hit hard, hit fast, hit often."

    A. Admiral Marc Mitscher

    B. General George Patton

    C. Admiral William Halsey

    D. General Walton Walker

92. "Because the people of our own American cities have been spared so far the cataclysm of aerial bombardment, we can only guess how our own people will behave when the time comes."

   A.   Admiral Harold Sallada

   B.   General Curtis LeMay

   C.   Secretary of State Cordell Hull

   D.   Colonel Pappy Boyington

93. "The outstanding achievement of this war in the field of joint undertakings was the perfection of amphibious operations, the most difficult of all operations in modern warfare."

   A.   Admiral Ernest King

   B.   General Holland Smith

   C.   Admiral Arthur Radford

   D.   General George Marshall

94. "I will break into Leyte Gulf and fight to the last man.... Would it not be shameful to have the fleet remaining intact while our nation perishes?"

   A.   Admiral Masa Arima

   B.   Admiral Kakuji Kakuta

   C.   Admiral Takeo Kurita

   D.   Admiral Teruhisa Komatsu

95. "In spite of intense efforts, the moment has drawn near when this front, already so heavily strained, will break."

    A.   General Wilhelm von Brandt

    B.   Field Marshal Gunther von Kluge

    C.   General Alfred Jodl

    D.   Field Marshal Paul von Kleist

96. "Hell is on us."

    A.   Prince Naruhiko Higashikuni

    B.   Field Marshal Mamoru Shigemitsu

    C.   Admiral Susumu Motoyama

    D.   Field Marshal Masayuki Tani

97. "Sixteen hours ago an American plane dropped one bomb on Hiroshima.... That bomb had more power than 20,000 tons of TNT.... With this bomb we have now added a new and revolutionary increase in destruction to supplement the growing power of our armed forces."

    A.   President Harry Truman

    B.   General Leslie Groves

    C.   President Franklin Roosevelt

    D.   J. Robert Oppenheimer

98. "Would it not be wondrous for this whole nation to be destroyed like a beautiful flower?"

    A.   Prince Naruhiko Higashikuni

    B.   Admiral Mitsumasa Yonai

    C.   General Korechika Anami

    D.   None of the above

99. "Our ships have been salvaged and are retiring at high speed toward the Japanese fleet."

    A.   Admiral Forrest Sherman

    B.   Admiral Chester Nimitz

    C.   Admiral Louis Denfeld

    D.   Admiral William Halsey

100. "Today the guns are silent. A great tragedy has ended. A great victory has been won."

    A.   Admiral Chester Nimitz

    B.   General Douglas MacArthur

    C.   Admiral Robert Carney

    D.   General Dwight Eisenhower

CHAPTER 6 ANSWERS

1.   C. President Franklin Roosevelt

2.   A. General George Patton

3.   C. Admiral Chester Nimitz

4.   D. Secretary of the Navy James Forrestal

5.   C. Secretary of the Navy Frank Knox

6.   B. Albert Speer

7.   A. Air Marshal Arthur Harris

8.   C. President George W. Bush

9.   D. President Ronald Reagan

10.   D. Admiral Karl Doenitz

11.   C. General Norman Cota

12.   B. Admiral Ernest King

13.   A. General Ira Eaker

14.   B. General Carl Spaatz

15.   A. General Jimmy Doolittle

16.   B. Heinrich Himmler

17.   A. Air Marshal Arthur Tedder

18.   D. General Curtis LeMay

19.   A. General Omar Bradley

20.   C. Admiral William Leahy

21.   D. Adolf Hitler

22. B. Admiral William Halsey

23. D. None of the above

24. D. General Henry Arnold

25. B. Field Marshal Erwin Rommel

26. A. Colonel Paul Tibbets

27. C. General Dwight Eisenhower

28. A. General Philippe Petain

29. B. Air Marshal Arthur Harris

30. D. General Heinz Guderian

31. C. Admiral Isoroku Yamamoto

32. B. General Percy Hobart

33. D. General Dwight Eisenhower

34. A. Colonel George Taylor

35. C. Adolf Hitler

36. A. General Alfred Jodl

37. A. Field Marshal Bernard Montgomery

38. C. General Jimmy Doolittle

39. D. Benito Mussolini

40. C. Emperor Hirohito

41. B. J. Robert Oppenheimer

42. D. General Joseph Stilwell

43. A. Reinhard Heydrich

44. D. General Franz Halder

45. A. Foreign Minister Vyacheslav Molotov

46. C. General James Gavin

47. A. General Tadamichi Kuribayashi

48. D. Prime Minister Winston Churchill

49. D. None of the above

50. B. President Franklin Roosevelt

51. A. General George Patton

52. D. General Douglas MacArthur

53. A. President Franklin Roosevelt

54. C. Field Marshal William Slim

55. A. Prime Minister Clement Attlee

56. B. Prime Minister Winston Churchill

57. C. Foreign Minister Galeazzo Ciano

58. C. Ernest Hemingway

59. A. Field Marshal Erwin Rommel

60. B. Field Marshal Friedrich Paulus

61. A. King George VI

62. C. General Bernard Freyberg

63. D. Admiral Erich Raeder

64. C. Admiral Seiichi Ito

65. B. General Mark Clark

66. D. Field Marshal Erhard Milch

67. C. Field Marshal Tomoyuki Yamashita

68. D. Admiral John Tovey

69. C. General Dwight Eisenhower

70. C. Adolf Hitler

71. D. None of the above

72. B. Vice President Henry Wallace

73. A. Hans Frank

74. A. Chiang Kai-shek

75. B. General George Marshall

76. D. Lieutenant Audie Murphy

77. C. Admiral Osami Nagano

78. B. Field Marshal Claude Auchinleck

79. C. Prime Minister Clement Attlee

80. C. General Douglas MacArthur

81. C. Lieutenant Audie Murphy

82. B. Lord Louis Mountbatten

83. D. Ambassador Joseph Grew

84. D. Prime Minister Neville Chamberlain

85. C. Admiral Isoroku Yamamoto

86. D. General Charles de Gaulle

87. B. Colonel Pappy Boyington

88. A. Joe Louis

89. D. Admiral Isoroku Yamamoto

90. B. Bill Mauldin

91. C. Admiral William Halsey

92. D. Colonel Pappy Boyington

93. A. Admiral Ernest King

94. C. Admiral Takeo Kurita

95. B. Field Marshal Gunther von Kluge

96. B. Field Marshal Mamoru Shigemitsu

97. A. President Harry Truman

98. C. General Korechika Anami

99. D. Admiral William Halsey

100. B. General Douglas MacArthur

CHAPTER 7
MILITARY ACRONYMS

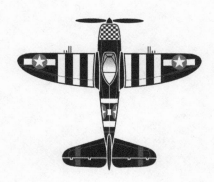

1. AA

    A. Air Ambulance

    B. Anti-Aircraft

    C. Air Assault

    D. None of the above

2. AAA

    A. Anti-Aircraft Assault

    B. Army Air Annex

    C. American Army Airborne

    D. Anti-Aircraft Artillery

3. AAF

    A. Asiatic Air Forces

    B. American Army Forces

    C. Anti-Aircraft Forces

    D. Army Air Forces

4. AAHQ

    A. Allied Air Headquarters

    B. Anti-Aircraft Headquarters

    C. Allied Army Headquarters

    D. Auxiliary Army Headquarters

5. ABDACOM

    A. American-British Demolition Command

    B. American-British-Dutch-Australian Supreme Command

    C. American-British-Dutch Army Command

    D. American-British-Dutch-Allied Command

6. ACM

    A. Army Court-Martial

    B. Air Combat Maneuvers

    C. Amphibious Command Manual

    D. Air Chief Marshal

7. AD

    A. Air Departure

    B. Aerial Decontamination

    C. Air Depot

    D. Aircraft Defense

8. AGF

    A. Artillery Grid Formation

    B. Army Ground Forces

    C. American Ground Fire

    D. Armored Ground Forces

9. ASW

    A. Administrative Search Warrant

    B. Army Standard Weapon

    C. Air to Surface Warfare

    D. Assistant Secretary of War

10. ATR

    A. Anti-Tank Rifle

    B. Air Target Reconnaissance

    C. Army Transport Recovery

    D. Airborne Technical Review

11. AVG

    A. American Volunteer Group

    B. Auxiliary Vehicle Glider

    C. American Volunteer Garrison

    D. Army Veterans Group

12. AVM

    A. Armored Vehicle Mine

    B. Air Vice Marshal

    C. Assault Vehicle Maneuvers

    D. Air Valor Medal

13. AW

    A. Advanced Weaponry

    B. Air Warning

    C. Automatic Weapon

    D. Advanced Warning

14. BAR

    A. Bentley Automatic Revolver

    B. British Aerial Reconnaissance

    C. Bureau of Aeronautics Report

    D. Browning Automatic Rifle

15. BD

    A. Base Data

    B. Battle Disposal

    C. Bomb Depot

    D. Battle Dress

16. BFM

    A. Belt-Fed Mechanism

    B. British Field Mess

    C. Battlefield Maneuvers

    D. Basic Field Manual

17. CCKW

    A. US Coast Watchers

    B. British Cargo Truck

    C. US Army Cargo Truck

    D. Canadian Cargo Truck

18. CE

    A. Combined Envelopment

    B. Corps of Engineers

    C. Chief Expenditure

    D. Canadian Expedition

19. CF

    A. Coastal Frontier

    B. Classified Files

    C. Coastal Forces

    D. Communist Forces

20. CG

    A. Camouflage Gear

    B. Cluster Grenade

    C. Classification Grade

    D. Coast Guard

21. CIGS

    A. Chief of the Imperial General Staff

    B. Canadian Imperial General Staff

    C. Chief Intelligence Group

    D. Confidential Intelligence Group Summary

22. CINCBPF

    A. Commander-in-Chief British Patrol Fleet

    B. Commander-in-Chief British Para-Military Force

    C. Commander-in-Chief British Patrol Force

    D. Commander-in-Chief British Pacific Fleet

23. CMH

    A. Command Mission Headquarters

    B. Congressional Medal of Honor

    C. Canadian Military Headquarters

    D. Combat Mission Headquarters

24. CNO

    A. Chief Noncommissioned Officer

    B. Controlled Naval Operation

    C. Chief of Naval Operations

    D. Commander of Naval Operations

25. CVB

    A. Aircraft Carrier, Escort

    B. Troop Carrier, Large

    C. Fleet Carrier, Escort

    D. Aircraft Carrier, Large

26. CVL

    A. Tank Carrier, Large

    B. Aircraft Carrier, Small

    C. Troop Carrier, Escort

    D. Aircraft Carrier, Large

27. CVS

    A. Carrier Suitability

    B. Seaplane Carrier

    C. Helicopter Carrier

    D. None of the above

28. CWO

    A. Chief Warrant Officer

    B. Combat Weapons Officer

    C. Contamination Warning Order

    D. Combined Warfare Office

29. CZ

    A. Coastal Zone

    B. Combat Zone

    C. Classified Zone

    D. Critical Zone

30. DFC

    A. Dutch Flying Corps

    B. Direct Flight Code

    C. Distinguished Flying Cross

    D. Divisional Forces Command

31. DOW

    A. Depth of Water

    B. Description of Wounds

    C. Died of Wounds

    D. Division of War

32. DSC

    A. Defense Security Corps

    B. Director of Staff College

    C. Defense Security Concerns

    D. Distinguished Service Cross

33. DSM

    A. Distinguished Service Medal

    B. Deputy Security Marshal

    C. Director of Staff Medicine

    D. Defense Security Mission

34. DSO

    A. Direct Security Order

    B. Distinguished Service Order

    C. Direct Sea Offensive

    D. Division of Seaplane Operations

35. DUKW

    A. Amphibious Tank

    B. Directory of United Kingdom Wounded

    C. Amphibious Truck

    D. None of the above

36. ETO

    A. European Theater Orders

    B. Electronic Training Operator

    C. Estimated Time Orders

    D. European Theater of Operations

37. FO

    A. Field Ordnance

    B. Flying Orders

    C. Forward Observer

    D. Field Orders

38. GHQ

    A. Ground Headquarters

    B. German Headquarters

    C. General Headquarters

    D. Garrison Headquarters

39. HB

    A. Harbor Base

    B. Heavy Bomber

    C. Helicopter Base

    D. None of the above

40. HMS

    A. Her Majesty's Service

    B. Heavy Mission Statistics

    C. His Majesty's Ship

    D. Hazardous Material Scale

41. IB

    A.   Incendiary Bomb

    B.   Independent Battalions

    C.   Input Basis

    D.   Island Base

42. IGD

    A.   Intelligence Growth Data

    B.   Inspector General's Department

    C.   Initial Glide Distribution

    D.   Intelligence Growth Division

43. JAG

    A.   Japanese Army General

    B.   Junior Air Grade

    C.   Judge Advocate General

    D.   Japanese Air Group

44. JWPC

    A.   Joint War Plans Committee

    B.   Japanese War Planning Conference

    C.   Joint War Production Commission

    D.   Japanese War Powers Committee

45. LCA

    A. Landing Craft, Army

    B. Limited Combatant Arrivals

    C. Lines of Communication Army

    D. Landing Craft, Assault

46. LCI

    A. Landing Craft Indicator

    B. Limited Combat Intelligence

    C. Landing Craft, Infantry

    D. Limited Craft Identification

47. LCM

    A. Lines of Communication Management

    B. Landing Craft, Marine

    C. Limited Combat Management

    D. Landing Craft, Mechanized

48. LCT

    A. Landing Craft, Tank

    B. Limited Combat Time

    C. Landing Craft Technician

    D. Limited Combat Training

49. LCV

    A. Limited Cost Variance

    B. Landing Craft, Vehicle

    C. London Communications Venue

    D. Land Combat Vehicle

50. LCVP

    A. Landing Craft, Large

    B. Landing Craft, Small

    C. Landing Craft, Vehicle and Personnel

    D. Landing Craft, Escort

51. LM

    A. Land Mass

    B. Light Mortar

    C. Level of Maintenance

    D. Legion of Merit

52. LMG

    A. Light Mortar Group

    B. Lower Military Grade

    C. Light Machine Gun

    D. None of the above

53. LP

    A. Light Pontoon

    B. Livens Projector

    C. Labor Platoon

    D. Lacerated Pelvis

54. LST

    A. Landing Ship, Tank

    B. Light Seaplane Tender

    C. Landing Ship Timing

    D. Light Standard Test

55. LSV

    A. Landing Support Vehicle

    B. Landing Ship, Vehicle

    C. Landing Support Escort

    D. Landing Ship, Escort

56. LVT

    A. Landing Support Tractor

    B. Landing Vehicle, Tracked

    C. Landing Support, Truck

    D. Landing Craft, Large

57. MA

    A.   Manchukuo Army

    B.   Magazine Assembly

    C.   Military Aviation

    D.   Military Attache

58. MC

    A.   Mobile Canteen

    B.   Mapping Camera

    C.   Military Cross

    D.   Marine Company

59. MH

    A.   Military Headquarters

    B.   Maritime Hazards

    C.   Military Housing

    D.   None of the above

60. MI

    A.   Marine Institute

    B.   Military Intelligence

    C.   Mine Inspection

    D.   Military Investigation

61. MSR

    A. Motorcycle Scout Report

    B. Medical Service Restrictions

    C. Mobile Surgical Resident

    D. Main Supply Road

62. MT

    A. Maritime Transport

    B. Mortar Target

    C. Motor Transport

    D. Marine Trailer

63. MTP

    A. Mobilization Training Program

    B. Military Transfer Protocol

    C. Medical Termination Program

    D. Mobile Training Procedures

64. NG

    A. National Guard

    B. Navigational Guide

    C. Navy Glider

    D. None of the above

65. OFM

    A. Office of Foreign Missions

    B. Operation FLYING MACHINE

    C. Ordnance Field Manual

    D. Operation FIRST MOON

66. OKW

    A. *Oberkommando der Wehrmacht*

    B. *Oberkommando des Heeres*

    C. *Oberstleutant der Wehrmacht*

    D. *Oberkommando der Marine*

67. OO

    A. Operation OSPREY

    B. Ordnance Officer

    C. Operation OCTAGON

    D. Observation Order

68. OP

    A. Observation Post

    B. Operation PALADIN

    C. Office of Personnel

    D. Operation PAWNBROKER

69. OSS

    A.   Operation SEA SWORD

    B.   Office of the Submarine Service

    C.   Operation SETTING SUN

    D.   Office of Strategic Services

70. OSW

    A.   Office of the Secretary of War

    B.   Operation SOUTHERN WIND

    C.   Office of Supply and Service

    D.   Operation STRATEGIC WARFARE

71. PD

    A.   Port of Debarkation

    B.   Parachute Deployment

    C.   Patrol Grid

    D.   Percussion Device

72. PE

    A.   Pistol Expert

    B.   Physical Emergency

    C.   Photographic Expert

    D.   Pillbox Explosives

73. PH

    A. Parachute Helmet

    B. Philippine Harbor

    C. Purple Heart

    D. Patrol Helicopter

74. PO

    A. Plan ORANGE

    B. Pilot Officer

    C. Plan OTTO

    D. None of the above

75. PT

    A. Patrol Target

    B. Pump Turret

    C. Pressure Tactics

    D. Primary Target

76. PTC

    A. Platoon Training Course

    B. Principal Transport Command

    C. Primary Training Center

    D. Pacific Theater Command

77. PTO

    A. Pacific Theater Ordnance

    B. Patrol Training Officer

    C. Pacific Theater of Operations

    D. Port Transportation Order

78. PW

    A. Primary Warfare

    B. Project Whirlwind

    C. Prisoner of War

    D. Plan White

79. QMG

    A. Queen's Military Guard

    B. Qualified Mission Guide

    C. Quartermaster General

    D. Qualified Military Goals

80. RA

    A. Regular Army

    B. Reconnaissance Aircraft

    C. Radar Antenna

    D. None of the above

81. RDF

   A. Royal Defense Force

   B. Radio Direction Finder

   C. Royal Destroyer Force

   D. Radar Detection Finder

82. SA

   A. Small Arms

   B. Sabotage Agent

   C. Sea and Air

   D. Screening Agent

83. SCM

   A. South Central Mediterranean

   B. Summary Court-Martial

   C. Special Carrier Mission

   D. Sea Corps Maneuvers

84. SS

   A. Submarine Squadron

   B. Staff Secretary

   C. Submersible Strategy

   D. Silver Star

85. SW

    A. Sea Worthy

    B. Selective Warfare

    C. Secretary of War

    D. Scout Wagon

86. TD

    A. Tank Destroyer

    B. Truck Division

    C. Transport Depot

    D. Tank Division

87. USW

    A. Underwater Sound Waves

    B. Unified Service

    C. Unrestricted Surface Warfare

    D. Undersecretary of War

88. VC

    A. Visual Correspondence

    B. Victory Cross

    C. Victim Count

    D. Victoria Cross

89. VF

    A. Victory Force

    B. Navy Fighter Squadron

    C. Victory Flag

    D. Naval Force

90. VMF

    A. Naval Munitions and Fuel

    B. Marine Fighter Squadron

    C. Volunteer Marine Force

    D. Navy Fighter Squadron

91. VMTB

    A. Marine Torpedo Bombing Squadron

    B. Navy Turbo Bomber

    C. Marine Torpedo Boat Squadron

    D. None of the above

92. WAAC

    A. Women's Auxiliary Air Corps

    B. Women's Army Air Corps

    C. Women's Air Acrobatic Corps

    D. Women's Army Auxiliary Corps

93. WAC

    A. Women's Army Conference

    B. Washington Aeronautics Commission

    C. World Allied Conference

    D. Women's Army Corps

94. WD

    A. War Depot

    B. Weapons Delivery

    C. War Department

    D. Work Detail

95. WDC

    A. Western Defense Council

    B. Wind Discharge Cone

    C. War Debt Council

    D. None of the above

96. WDCSA

    A. Chief of Staff US Air Corps

    B. Washington Defense Command South Atlantic

    C. Chief of Staff US Air Force

    D. War Department Chief of Staff US Army

97. WIA

    A. Wartime Investment Act

    B. War in Asia

    C. Wounded in Action

    D. Warfare Initiative Act

98. WO

    A. Weather Observer

    B. Work Order

    C. Warrant Officer

    D. War Operations

99. WPD

    A. War Plans Division

    B. Naval Procurement Division

    C. War Production Department

    D. Wartime Placement Division

100. YFD

    A. Fleet Air Arm

    B. Aircraft Transportation Barge

    C. Bureau of Fleet Designation

    D. Floating Dry Dock

CHAPTER 7 ANSWERS

1. B. Anti-Aircraft

2. D. Anti-Aircraft Artillery

3. D. Army Air Forces

4. A. Allied Air Headquarters

5. B. American-British-Dutch-Australian Supreme Command

6. D. Air Chief Marshal

7. C. Air Depot

8. B. Army Ground Forces

9. D. Assistant Secretary of War

10. A. Anti-Tank Rifle

11. A. American Volunteer Group

12. B. Air Vice Marshal

13. C. Automatic Weapon

14. D. Browning Automatic Rifle

15. D. Battle Dress

16. D. Basic Field Manual

17. C. US Army Cargo Truck

18. B. Corps of Engineers

19. A. Coastal Frontier

20. D. Coast Guard

21. A. Chief of the Imperial General Staff

22. D. Commander-in-Chief British Pacific Fleet

23. B. Congressional Medal of Honor

24. C. Chief of Naval Operations

25. D. Aircraft Carrier, Large

26. B. Aircraft Carrier, Small

27. B. Seaplane Carrier

28. A. Chief Warrant Officer

29. B. Combat Zone

30. C. Distinguished Flying Cross

31. C. Died of Wounds

32. D. Distinguished Service Cross

33. A. Distinguished Service Medal

34. B. Distinguished Service Order

35. C. Amphibious Truck

36. D. European Theater of Operations

37. C. Forward Observer

38. C. General Headquarters

39. B. Heavy Bomber

40. C. His Majesty's Ship

41. A. Incendiary Bomb

42. B. Inspector General's Department

43. C. Judge Advocate General

44. A. Joint War Plans Committee

45. D. Landing Craft, Assault

46. C. Landing Craft, Infantry

47. D. Landing Craft, Mechanized

48. A. Landing Craft, Tank

49. B. Landing Craft, Vehicle

50. C. Landing Craft, Vehicle and Personnel

51. D. Legion of Merit

52. C. Light Machine Gun

53. B. Livens Projector

54. A. Landing Ship, Tank

55. B. Landing Ship, Vehicle

56. B. Landing Vehicle, Tracked

57. D. Military Attache

58. C. Military Cross

59. A. Military Headquarters

60. B. Military Intelligence

61. D. Main Supply Road

62. C. Motor Transport

63. A. Mobilization Training Program

64. A. National Guard

65. C. Ordnance Field Manual

66. A. *Oberkommando der Wehrmacht*

67. B. Ordnance Officer

68. A. Observation Post

69. D. Office of Strategic Services

70. A. Office of the Secretary of War

71. A. Port of Debarkation

72. A. Pistol Expert

73. C. Purple Heart

74. D. None of the above

75. D. Primary Target

76. C. Primary Training Center

77. C. Pacific Theater of Operations

78. C. Prisoner of War

79. C. Quartermaster General

80. A. Regular Army

81. B. Radio Direction Finder

82. A. Small Arms

83. B. Summary Court-Martial

84. D. Silver Star

85. C. Secretary of War

86. A. Tank Destroyer

87. D. Undersecretary of War

88. D. Victoria Cross

89. B. Navy Fighter Squadron

90. B. Marine Fighter Squadron

91. A. Marine Torpedo Bombing Squadron

92. D. Women's Army Auxiliary Corps

93. D. Women's Army Corps

94. C. War Department

95. D. None of the above

96. D. War Department Chief of Staff US Army

97. C. Wounded in Action

98. C. Warrant Officer

99. A. War Plans Division

100. D. Floating Dry Dock

CHAPTER 8
GI SLANG

1. Army Banjo

    A. Shovel

    B. Guitar

    C. Rifle

    D. None of the above

2. Army Chicken

    A. Steak

    B. Meatloaf

    C. Veal

    D. Franks and beans

3. Army Strawberries

    A. Bullets

    B. Raisins

    C. Prunes

    D. Nurses

4. Ash Can

    A. Chewing tobacco

    B. Depth charge

    C. M3 Stuart tank

    D. Ashtray

5. Asparagus Stick

    A. German hand grenade

    B. Dynamite

    C. Submarine periscope

    D. Thermometer

6. Axle Grease

    A. Butter

    B. Vaseline

    C. Cottage cheese

    D. Molasses

7. Bags of Mystery

    A. Salami

    B. Pepperoni

    C. Letters

    D. Sausages

8. Barracks Lawyer

    A. Medic

    B. Field manual

    C. Know-it-all

    D. Drill sergeant

9. Battery Acid

    A. Powdered milk

    B. Gin

    C. Lemonade powder

    D. Bourbon

10. Bedpan Commando

    A. Navy doctor

    B. Wounded GI

    C. Army doctor

    D. Corpsman

11. Bite the Dust

    A. Killed

    B. Demoted

    C. Punished

    D. Crippled

12. Blanket Drill

    A. Court-martial

    B. Target practice

    C. Sexual encounter

    D. Nap

13. Blind Flying

    A.   Visual flight

    B.   Assaulting an enemy position

    C.   Night patrol

    D.   Blind date

14. Blister Foot

    A.   Sergeant-major

    B.   Podiatrist

    C.   Infantryman

    D.   Recruit

15. Body Snatcher

    A.   Troublemaker

    B.   Stretcher-bearer

    C.   Grave digger

    D.   None of the above

16. Bog-Pocket

    A.   Tightwad

    B.   Slob

    C.   Big-time spender

    D.   Sharp dresser

17. Bottled Sunshine

    A. Grapefruit juice

    B. Orange juice

    C. Beer

    D. Wine

18. Broad with Canned Goods

    A. Virgin

    B. Waitress

    C. Prostitute

    D. Girlfriend

19. Browned-Off

    A. Drunk

    B. Annoyed

    C. Dishonorably discharged

    D. Suntanned

20. Brush

    A. Comb

    B. Rake

    C. Mustache

    D. Burp gun

21. Bubble Dancing

    A. Drowning

    B. Skinny-dipping

    C. Dishwashing

    D. Farting in the bathtub

22. Bug Juice

    A. Diesel fuel

    B. Moonshine

    C. Dirty water

    D. Insect repellent

23. C-Ration

    A. Penicillin

    B. Diarrhea

    C. Vomit

    D. Canned food

24. Canary

    A. Enemy aircraft

    B. Carrier pigeon

    C. Attractive woman

    D. Sweetheart

25. Canned Morale

    A. Movie

    B. Whiskey

    C. Prayer

    D. USO show

26. Cast-Iron Bathtub

    A. PT boat

    B. Aircraft carrier

    C. Submarine

    D. Battleship

27. Cat

    A. Russian sniper

    B. Amphibious vehicle

    C. Loose woman

    D. Catalina flying boat

28. Cat's Beer

    A. Milk

    B. Urine

    C. Water

    D. Coffee

29. Chatterbox

    A. Machine gun

    B. Chain smoker

    C. Ammunition box

    D. None of the above

30. Cheaters

    A. Glasses

    B. Suspenders

    C. Boots

    D. Socks

31. Chicken Berry

    A. Hen

    B. Egg

    C. Gizzard

    D. Rooster

32. Chicken Colonel

    A. Cowardly officer

    B. Full colonel

    C. Farmboy

    D. Lieutenant colonel

33. Coffee Cooler

    A. Loafer

    B. Cream

    C. Liar

    D. Cognac

34. Collision Mats

    A. Toast

    B. Waffles

    C. Kleenex

    D. Gloves

35. Corner Turner

    A. Novel

    B. Steering wheel

    C. Deserter

    D. Magazine

36. D-Ration

    A. Cereal

    B. Oatmeal

    C. Explosives

    D. Military chocolate

37. Devil Beater

    A. Bulldozer

    B. Spade

    C. Womanizer

    D. Chaplain

38. Devil's Piano

    A. Contact mine

    B. Machine gun

    C. Katyusha rocket launcher

    D. Tiger II tank

39. Do-Re-Mi

    A. Money

    B. Music

    C. Friends

    D. Triplets

40. Dogface

    A. Ugly woman

    B. Infantryman

    C. Paratrooper

    D. Canine handler

41. Dumbo

    A.   Tank

    B.   Career officer

    C.   Life raft

    D.   None of the above

42. File 13

    A.   Latrine

    B.   Fireplace

    C.   Wastebasket

    D.   Foxhole

43. Fruit Salad

    A.   Medal of Honor

    B.   Gangrene

    C.   Frostbite

    D.   Campaign ribbons

44. Gertrude

    A.   German woman

    B.   Wife

    C.   Office clerk

    D.   General's driver

45. Jesus

    A. General

    B. Helmet

    C. Rifle

    D. Chaplain

46. Joe

    A. Soldier

    B. Dentist

    C. Surgeon

    D. Buddy

47. Gink

    A. Glue

    B. Stupid person

    C. Noncommissioned officer

    D. Lamb stew

48. Grandma Gear

    A. Underwear

    B. Dressing gown

    C. Low gear

    D. Homemade cookies

49. Gravel Agitator

    A. Foot soldier

    B. M4 Sherman tank

    C. Tractor

    D. M3 Half-track

50. Hanger Warrior

    A. Chief signalman

    B. Aircraft mechanic

    C. Machinist's mate

    D. Carrier pilot

51. Hash Burner

    A. Flamethrower

    B. Hamburger

    C. Stove

    D. Cook

52. Jawbreakers

    A. Diamonds

    B. Candy

    C. Ice

    D. Biscuits

53. Joe

    A. Best friend

    B. Coffee

    C. Tea

    D. Cigarettes

54. Juice Jerker

    A. Electrician

    B. Petty officer

    C. Mess attendant

    D. Radio operator

55. Kite

    A. Troop glider

    B. Haircut

    C. Airplane

    D. None of the above

56. Lead Poisoning

    A. Tin plate

    B. Infection

    C. Artillery shell

    D. Bullet

57. Looseners

    A. Scissors

    B. Tweezers

    C. Suppositories

    D. Prunes

58. Mae West

    A. Flotation vest

    B. Fuel depot

    C. Brassiere

    D. Inflatable raft

59. Misery Pipe

    A. Bazooka

    B. Cigar

    C. Trumpet

    D. Bugle

60. Mitt Flopper

    A. Catcher's glove

    B. Traitor

    C. Yes-man

    D. Skillet

61. Monkey Clothes

    A. Overalls

    B. Street clothes

    C. Full-dress uniform

    D. Medical gown

62. Mousetrap

    A. Sniper

    B. Cheese

    C. Anti-tank mine

    D. Submarine

63. Nut Buster

    A. Mechanic

    B. Wrench

    C. Tight pants

    D. Insect

64. On-a-Toot

    A. Unconscious

    B. Drunk

    C. Lonely

    D. Wounded

65. Pep Tire

    A. Pancake

    B. Doughnut

    C. Record

    D. Card game

66. Pig Snout

    A. Gas mask

    B. Ham sandwich

    C. Ugly nurse

    D. Gas can

67. Pineapple

    A. Prophylactic

    B. Artillery shell

    C. Grenade

    D. Atomic bomb

68. Pocket Lettuce

    A. Money

    B. Sandwich

    C. Lint

    D. Playing cards

69. Podunk

    A. Soldier's hometown

    B. Dead end

    C. The big city

    D. A convoy

70. Popsicle

    A. Bangalore torpedo

    B. Willys jeep

    C. Motorcycle

    D. None of the above

71. Popsie

    A. Explosion

    B. Popsicle

    C. Dad

    D. Girlfriend

72. Rack Happy

    A. Bored

    B. Scared

    C. Energetic

    D. Tired

73. Ratzy

    A. Communist

    B. Fascist

    C. Imperialist

    D. German soldier

74. Retread

    A. Prisoner of war

    B. Tank commander

    C. Older recruit

    D. Veteran serving in World War II

75. Rookie

    A. Recruit

    B. Italian soldier

    C. Second lieutenant

    D. Virgin

76. Sad Sack

    A. Unlucky soldier

    B. Oil drum

    C. Unmade bunk

    D. Japanese pilot

77. Saltwater Cowboy

    A. Marine

    B. Seabee

    C. Frogman

    D. Commando

78. Sea Dust

    A. Smoke

    B. Fog

    C. Baking soda

    D. Salt

79. Section 8

    A. Military discharge

    B. Guard duty

    C. High fever

    D. Enlistment Act

80. Serum

    A. Moonshine

    B. Cough syrup

    C. Pep talk

    D. Intoxicating beverage

81. Shack Man

    A. Married man

    B. Spy

    C. Doctor

    D. Informer

82. Sheila

    A. Stray dog

    B. Girlfriend

    C. Sister

    D. French woman

83. Shingles

    A. Boots

    B. Toast

    C. Hemorrhoids

    D. Toilet paper

84. Short Arm

    A. Left-handed pitcher

    B. Amputee

    C. Penis

    D. Thief

85. Shrapnel

    A. Grapefruit

    B. String beans

    C. Bananas

    D. Asparagus

86. Shutters

    A. Warm compresses

    B. Sleeping pills

    C. Goggles

    D. Sunglasses

87. Skin

    A. Handshake

    B. Poker winnings

    C. Monthly pay

    D. Army reprimand

88. Sky Scout

    A. Chaplain

    B. Flying Fortress

    C. Parachute

    D. Barrage balloon

89. Snore Sack

    A. Tent

    B. Sleeping bag

    C. Bed

    D. Duffle bag

90. Son of Mars

    A. Complainer

    B. Candy bar

    C. Soldier

    D. None of the above

91. Soup

    A. Snow

    B. Fog

    C. Gravy

    D. Sleet

92. Sugar Report

    A. Sweetheart letter

    B. Divorce

    C. Birthday cake

    D. Two-day pass

93. Superman Suit

    A.   Underwear

    B.   Overalls

    C.   Full-dress uniform

    D.   Swim trunks

94. Swacked

    A.   Married

    B.   Silly

    C.   Intoxicated

    D.   Sleepy

95. Table Muscle

    A.   Tough guy

    B.   Company boxer

    C.   Arm wrestler

    D.   Fat

96. Taxi-Up

    A.   Fall back

    B.   Get together

    C.   Move forward

    D.   Come here

97. Tiger Meat

    A. Beef

    B. Chicken

    C. Spam

    D. Veal

98. Tin Pickle

    A. Torpedo

    B. Artillery shell

    C. Bazooka

    D. Cigar

99. Uncle Sam's Party

    A. Fourth of July

    B. V-E Day

    C. Payday

    D. Furlough

100. USO Commando

    A. Musician

    B. Hometown hero

    C. Bandleader

    D. Comedian

CHAPTER 8 ANSWERS

1. A. Shovel

2. D. Franks and beans

3. C. Prunes

4. B. Depth charge

5. C. Submarine periscope

6. A. Butter

7. D. Sausages

8. C. Know-it-all

9. C. Lemonade powder

10. D. Corpsman

11. A. Killed

12. D. Nap

13. D. Blind date

14. C. Infantryman

15. B. Stretcher-bearer

16. A. Tightwad

17. C. Beer

18. A. Virgin

19. B. Annoyed

20. C. Mustache

21. C. Dishwashing

22. D. Insect repellent

23. D. Canned food

24. C. Attractive woman

25. A. Movie

26. D. Battleship

27. D. Catalina flying boat

28. A. Milk

29. A. Machine gun

30. A. Glasses

31. B. Egg

32. B. Full colonel

33. A. Loafer

34. B. Waffles

35. C. Deserter

36. D. Military chocolate

37. D. Chaplain

38. B. Machine gun

39. A. Money

40. B. Infantryman

41. D. None of the above

42. C. Wastebasket

43. D. Campaign ribbons

44. C. Office clerk

45. D. Chaplain

46. A. Soldier

47. B. Stupid person

48. C. Low gear

49. A. Foot soldier

50. B. Aircraft mechanic

51. D. Cook

52. D. Biscuits

53. B. Coffee

54. A. Electrician

55. C. Airplane

56. D. Bullet

57. D. Prunes

58. A. Flotation vest

59. D. Bugle

60. C. Yes-man

61. C. Full-dress uniform

62. D. Submarine

63. A. Mechanic

64. B. Drunk

65. B. Doughnut

66. A. Gas mask

67. C. Grenade

68. A. Money

69. A. Soldier's hometown

70. C. Motorcycle

71. D. Girlfriend

72. A. Bored

73. D. German soldier

74. D. Veteran serving in World War II

75. A. Recruit

76. A. Unlucky soldier

77. A. Marine

78. D. Salt

79. A. Military discharge

80. D. Intoxicating beverage

81. A. Married man

82. B. Girlfriend

83. B. Toast

84. C. Penis

85. A. Grapefruit

86. B. Sleeping pills

87. D. Army reprimand

88. A. Chaplain

89. B. Sleeping bag

90. C. Soldier

91. B. Fog

92. A. Sweetheart letter

93. A. Underwear

94. C. Intoxicated

95. D. Fat

96. D. Come here

97. A. Beef

98. A. Torpedo

99. C. Payday

100. B. Hometown hero

CHAPTER 9

FILMS

CHAPTER 9

PLANS

1. Gregory Peck received an Academy Award nomination for his portrayal of a tough-minded general who takes command of a B-17 bomb group in

   A. *Twelve O'Clock High*

   B. *Command Decision*

   C. *Thirty Seconds Over Tokyo*

   D. *Flying Tigers*

2. This war-hero-turned-actor starred in the 1955 biopic *To Hell and Back.*

   A. James Stewart

   B. Audie Murphy

   C. Clark Gable

   D. Tyrone Power

3. "A Man with the Heart of a Nation" was the tagline for this movie.

   A. *The Man Who Never Was*

   B. *Darkest Hour*

   C. *Hitler: The Last Ten Days*

   D. *Give 'Em Hell, Harry!*

4. The following war films won the Oscar for Best Picture *except*

   A. *Patton*

   B. *Schindler's List*

   C. *Bridge on the River Kwai*

   D. *Saving Private Ryan*

5. Who took the role of Erwin Rommel in the 1951 movie *The Desert Fox*?

    A. Michael Rennie

    B. James Mason

    C. Richard Burton

    D. Rex Harrison

6. In this film, directed by John Huston, a Catholic nun and a US Marine are stranded on a Japanese-held island.

    A. *The Bells of St. Mary's*

    B. *God Is My Co-Pilot*

    C. *Heaven Knows Mr. Allison*

    D. *Between Heaven and Hell*

7. Who portrayed Field Marshal Gerd von Rundstedt in *A Bridge Too Far*?

    A. Klaus Kinski

    B. Gert Frobe

    C. Wolfgang Preiss

    D. None of the above

8. This 1990 film chronicled the twenty-fifth and final mission of a B-17 crew.

    A. *The War Lovers*

    B. *Hell Is for Heroes*

    C. *Memphis Belle*

    D. *The Glory Guys*

9. Which movie's tagline was "When the Hunters Become the Hunted"?

    A. *Up Periscope!*

    B. *Torpedo Run*

    C. *Das Boot*

    D. *Wolves of the Deep*

10. Legendary filmmaker _____ directed the propaganda series *Why We Fight*.

    A. John Ford

    B. William Wellman

    C. Howard Hawks

    D. Frank Capra

11. In *Von Ryan's Express,* which actor said, "You'll get your Iron Cross now, Von Ryan!"

    A. Brad Dexter

    B. Frank Sinatra

    C. Trevor Howard

    D. Edward Mulhare

12. He played General Theodore Roosevelt Jr. in *The Longest Day* and Admiral Chester Nimitz in *Midway*.

    A. Robert Mitchum

    B. Glenn Ford

    C. Jason Robards

    D. Henry Fonda

13. Which future politician starred in the 1949 classic *Battleground*?

    A.   Wendell Corey

    B.   Ronald Reagan

    C.   Van Johnson

    D.   George Murphy

14. This composer scored the 1961 film *The Guns of Navarone*.

    A.   Dimitri Tiomkin

    B.   Mitch Miller

    C.   James Horner

    D.   Henry Mancini

15. In *The Story of GI Joe*, who portrayed war correspondent Ernie Pyle?

    A.   William Powell

    B.   Spencer Tracy

    C.   Burgess Meredith

    D.   Humphrey Bogart

16. Schofield Barracks was the setting for which Academy Award-winning film?

    A.   *On the Beach*

    B.   *From Here to Eternity*

    C.   *Tour of Duty*

    D.   None of the above

17. Name the legendary crooner who starred with Marlon Brando and Montgomery Clift in *The Young Lions*.

    A. Nat King Cole

    B. Tony Bennett

    C. Dean Martin

    D. Bing Crosby

18. This leading man played General Frank Merrill in the 1962 motion picture *Merrill's Marauders*.

    A. George Segal

    B. Rock Hudson

    C. George Peppard

    D. Jeff Chandler

19. "When 400,000 Men Couldn't Get Home, Home Came for Them" was the tagline for this motion picture.

    A. *Anzio*

    B. *Stalingrad*

    C. *Dunkirk*

    D. *Ten Seconds to Hell*

20. In how many World War II films did veteran actor Richard Jaeckel appear?

    A. Ten

    B. Thirteen

    C. Sixteen

    D. Nineteen

21. He portrayed future President John F. Kennedy in *PT-109*.

    A. Cliff Robertson

    B. Robert Redford

    C. Ty Hardin

    D. Edd Byrnes

22. Which of the following leading men did not star in *The Longest Day*?

    A. Robert Ryan

    B. Kirk Douglas

    C. Robert Mitchum

    D. Sean Connery

23. In *Patton*, which actor said, "It's not important for them to know. It's only important for me to know."

    A. George C. Scott

    B. Karl Malden

    C. Michael Strong

    D. Karl Michael Vogler

24. The companion film to Clint Eastwood's Oscar-nominated *Flags of Our Fathers* was

    A. *Sands of Iwo Jima*

    B. *Halls of Montezuma*

    C. *Letters from Iwo Jima*

    D. *None But the Brave*

25. He won an Academy Award for his portrayal of defense attorney Hans Rolfe in *Judgment at Nuremberg*.

    A. Marlon Brando

    B. Christopher Plummer

    C. Maximilian Schell

    D. Curt Jurgens

26. Which actor took the role of a mentally unstable naval officer in *The Caine Mutiny*?

    A. Fred McMurray

    B. Humphrey Bogart

    C. Jose Ferrer

    D. Van Johnson

27. James Cagney starred in this 1960 biographical account of Admiral William Halsey.

    A. *The Gallant Hours*

    B. *He Stood Alone*

    C. *The Gallant Men*

    D. *Guadalcanal Diary*

28. In *Reach for the Sky*, Kenneth More portrayed a legless RAF fighter ace. Who was he?

    A. Johnnie Johnson

    B. Brendan Finucane

    C. Douglas Bader

    D. George Buerling

29. Which member of a famous musical duo made his acting debut in *Catch-22*?

  A.   Sonny Bono

  B.   Art Garfunkel

  C.   Daryl Hall

  D.   Phil Everly

30. In this 1964 comedy, Don Knotts plays a man turned fish who helps the US Navy locate and destroy German submarines.

  A.   *The Amazing Kingfish*

  B.   *A Fish Called Wanda*

  C.   *The Incredible Mr. Limpet*

  D.   *Flipper Joins the Navy*

31. Which John Wayne war film came first?

  A.   *They Were Expendable*

  B.   *Flying Tigers*

  C.   *Back to Bataan*

  D.   *The Fighting Seabees*

32. This English actor graduated from the Royal Military College, Sandhurst, and served with the British Army during World War II.

  A.   Leslie Howard

  B.   Laurence Olivier

  C.   David Niven

  D.   Noel Coward

33. He portrayed a British officer who matched wits with his Japanese counterpart in a jungle prison camp.

    A.   Richard Burton

    B.   Anthony Quayle

    C.   Alec Guinness

    D.   Jack Hawkins

34. This was the first wartime film to win the Oscar for Best Picture.

    A.   *Since You Went Away*

    B.   *The Best Years of Our Lives*

    C.   *Casablanca*

    D.   *Watch on the Rhine*

35. Which movie inspired the *Ensign Pulver* sequel?

    A.   *Operation Petticoat*

    B.   *Away All Ships*

    C.   *Mr. Roberts*

    D.   *The Wackiest Ship in the Army*

36. He played the bookkeeper opposite Liam Neeson in *Schindler's List*.

    A.   Ben Kingsley

    B.   Christoph Waltz

    C.   Jude Law

    D.   Ralph Fiennes

37. "Their Mission: Stop the Nazis from Developing the Atomic Bomb" was the tagline for

    A.   *Race for the Bomb*

    B.   *The Manhattan Project*

    C.   *Fat Man and Little Boy*

    D.   *The Heroes of Telemark*

38. Which type of motorcycle did Steve McQueen ride in *The Great Escape?*

    A.   Ariel Square Four

    B.   Triumph TR6 Trophy

    C.   BMW R60/2

    D.   Norton Commando

39. This 1957 film pitted a U-boat commander against the captain of a US destroyer in the South Atlantic.

    A.   *The Enemy Below*

    B.   *U-571*

    C.   *Das Boot*

    D.   None of the above

40. Funnyman Don Rickles made his film debut in this tense naval drama.

    A.   *Advance to the Rear*

    B.   *Run Silent Run Deep*

    C.   *Operation Pacific*

    D.   *Murphy's War*

41. This Hollywood tough guy served as a tail gunner in the US Army Air Corps and was awarded the Purple Heart.

    A. Ernest Borgnine

    B. Paul Newman

    C. Charles Bronson

    D. Rod Steiger

42. Which World War II comedy included characters with names like "Big Joe," "Crapgame," and "Oddball"?

    A. *Catch-22*

    B. *Kelly's Heroes*

    C. *Castle Keep*

    D. *Which Way to the Front?*

43. This movie's tagline was "Every Man Fights His Own War."

    A. *The Thin Red Line*

    B. *Hell in the Pacific*

    C. *Armored Command*

    D. *The Big Red One*

44. Which future president signed Major Clark Gable's US Army discharge papers in 1944?

    A. Dwight Eisenhower

    B. Ronald Reagan

    C. Harry Truman

    D. Richard Nixon

45. A *Wehrmacht* officer is suspected of murdering prostitutes in this 1967 thriller.

    A. *The Night of the Generals*

    B. *Double Cross*

    C. *The Unlikely Killer*

    D. *Murder in Warsaw*

46. Which were the names of the three tunnels dug by the Allied POWs in *The Great Escape*?

    A. "Tom, Jerry, and Terry"

    B. "Moe, Larry, and Curly"

    C. "Tom, Dick, and Harry"

    D. "Manny, Moe, and Jack"

47. He directed the 1965 film *In Harm's Way*.

    A. William Wyler

    B. Howard Hawks

    C. Otto Preminger

    D. John Gullermin

48. William Powell and Jack Lemmon starred opposite Henry Fonda in this 1955 John Ford classic.

    A. *Mr. Roberts*

    B. *Imitation General*

    C. *The Long Gray Line*

    D. *What Price Glory*

49. In *The Longest Day*, which actor said, "He's dead. I'm crippled. You're lost. Do you suppose it's always like that? I mean war."

    A. Richard Burton

    B. Peter Lawford

    C. Robert Ryan

    D. Mel Ferrer

50. "At the Front Lines of Life, Near the End of Innocence, Came the Beginning of Manhood" was this film's tagline.

    A. *A Midnight Clear*

    B. *Saints and Sinners*

    C. *Army of Shadows*

    D. *Cross of Iron*

51. A Grammy Award-winning recording artist, _____ played Private Corby in the 1962 film *Hell Is for Heroes*.

    A. James Darren

    B. Del Shannon

    C. Bobby Darin

    D. Gene Pitney

52. Which real-life member of the 101ˢᵗ Airborne Division was the inspiration for Steven Spielberg's *Saving Private Ryan?*

    A. Edward "Tank" Sullivan

    B. James "Irish" Ryan

    C. Frederick "Fritz" Niland

    D. Henry "Moose" Morehouse

53. This British actor portrayed Nikita Khrushchev in *Enemy at the Gates*.

    A. Edward Fox

    B. Daniel Craig

    C. Bob Hoskins

    D. Jude Law

54. Which film had the tagline "When the Order Came to Retreat, One Man Stayed"?

    A. *Suicide Battalion*

    B. *Hacksaw Ridge*

    C. *The Young Lions*

    D. *Destiny of a Man*

55. In *The Great Escape*, who played "the Forger"?

    A. Richard Attenborough

    B. James Garner

    C. Donald Pleasence

    D. James Coburn

56. Adolf Hitler offered a $5,000 bounty to anyone who captured this Hollywood icon.

    A. Clark Gable

    B. John Wayne

    C. Gary Cooper

    D. Henry Fonda

57. Which of these war films won the most Oscars?

    A. *Stalag 17*

    B. *Patton*

    C. *Black Hawk Down*

    D. *Pork Chop Hill*

58. His directorial debut was the 1943 motion picture *Destination Tokyo*.

    A. Samuel Fuller

    B. Delmer Daves

    C. Sam Peckinpah

    D. Billy Wilder

59. "Music Was His Passion. Survival Was His Masterpiece" was this motion picture's tagline.

    A. *Life Is Beautiful*

    B. *Phoenix*

    C. *When Trumpets Fade*

    D. *The Pianist*

60. How many convicts in *The Dirty Dozen* survived the mission?

    A. Zero

    B. One

    C. Three

    D. None of the above

61. In *Pearl Harbor*, who portrayed Seaman First Class Dorian Miller, the first African American to be awarded the Navy Cross for heroism?

    A.   Will Smith

    B.   Forest Whitaker

    C.   Cuba Gooding Jr.

    D.   Denzel Washington

62. Which country music legend almost starred in *Saving Private Ryan*?

    A.   Willie Nelson

    B.   Garth Brooks

    C.   Tim McGraw

    D.   Blake Shelton

63. This was the name of Humphrey Bogart's tank in the wartime film *Sahara*.

    A.   "Josephine"

    B.   "Lulu Belle"

    C.   "Rosie"

    D.   "Clara Belle"

64. Which was the setting for the 2004 foreign film *Downfall*?

    A.   A bombed-out factory in Stalingrad

    B.   Hitler's Berlin bunker

    C.   A German U-boat in the North Atlantic

    D.   Rommel's headquarters in North Africa

65. The title of the 1970 docudrama *Tora! Tora! Tora!* means

    A.   Tiger! Tiger! Tiger!

    B.   Attack! Attack! Attack!

    C.   Surprise! Surprise! Surprise!

    D.   Go! Go! Go!

66. Which was the highest-grossing war film of all time and winner of the Best Picture Oscar?

    A.   *The Bridges of Toko-Ri*

    B.   *MacArthur*

    C.   *The Best Years of Our Lives*

    D.   *Schindler's List*

67. This movie's tagline was "He Needed to Trust Her with His Secret. She Needed to Trust Him with Her Life."

    A.   *Shining Through*

    B.   *A Walk in the Sun*

    C.   *Mission to Lisbon*

    D.   *Rendezvous in Berlin*

68. He portrayed Colonel Claus von Stauffenberg (with an American accent) in *Valkyrie*.

    A.   Armie Hammer

    B.   Tom Cruise

    C.   Ben Affleck

    D.   Matthew McConaughey

69. Which secret does Donald Sutherland keep from Kate Nelligan and Christopher Cazenove in *Eye of the Needle*?

    A. He's an army deserter.

    B. He was sent to assassinate Hitler.

    C. He's a Russian spy.

    D. He was sent to assassinate Churchill.

70. In *The Train*, Burt Lancaster prevents the Germans from smuggling _____ out of France.

    A. Jews

    B. weapons

    C. uranium

    D. works of art

71. Who played the role of General Hideki Tojo in *Emperor*?

    A. Masato Ibu

    B. Kengo Hasuo

    C. Shohei Hino

    D. Takataro Kataoka

72. The residents of an English village are invaded by German paratroopers in

    A. *Operation Crossbow*

    B. *Too Late the Hero*

    C. *The Eagle Has Landed*

    D. *Dangerous Crossing*

73. Which actor impersonated the voice of President Franklin Roosevelt in *Darkest Hour*?

    A. Bill Murray

    B. Edward Hermann

    C. David Strathairn

    D. John Voight

74. "In a Time of Conflict, Innocence Was Lost" was the tagline for this film.

    A. *Charlotte Gray*

    B. *The War Bride*

    C. *December*

    D. *The Bridge at Remagen*

75. The *Halls of Montezuma* marked the movie debut of

    A. Richard Boone and Robert Wagner

    B. Karl Malden and Jack Palance

    C. Jack Webb and Neville Brand

    D. Neville Brand and Richard Widmark

76. Which film was full of historical inaccuracies and publicly denounced by former President Dwight Eisenhower?

    A. *King Rat*

    B. *Is Paris Burning?*

    C. *The Longest Day*

    D. *Battle of the Bulge*

77. The comedic duo of Abbott and Costello starred as US Army recruits in this World War II-era farce.

    A. *Basic Training*

    B. *Caught in the Draft*

    C. *Buck Privates*

    D. None of the above

78. Best known for his comedic roles, he impersonated the voice of Winston Churchill in *The Man Who Never Was*.

    A. Terry Thomas

    B. Stan Laurel

    C. Peter Sellers

    D. John Cleese

79. Which teen idol wrote the theme song to *The Longest Day*?

    A. Paul Anka

    B. Bobby Rydell

    C. Frankie Avalon

    D. Neil Sedaka

80. In *The Bridge on the River Kwai*, which actor said, "Do not speak to me of rules. This is not a game of cricket!"

    A. Jack Hawkins

    B. William Holden

    C. Sessue Hayakawa

    D. Alec Guinness

81. Who took the role of General Leslie Groves in *Fat Man and Little Boy*?

    A. Dustin Hoffman

    B. Paul Newman

    C. Robert Redford

    D. John Lithgow

82. The tagline for this 1960 docudrama was "Personal! Powerful! Human! Heroic!"

    A. *Sink the Bismarck!*

    B. *The Tommies Fight On*

    C. *Damn the Defiant!*

    D. *The Desert Rats*

83. On which island does *The Thin Red Line* take place?

    A. Okinawa

    B. Tarawa

    C. Peleliu

    D. Guadalcanal

84. Which legendary film director starred as *Oberst* von Scherbach in *Stalag 17*?

    A. Fritz Lang

    B. Otto Preminger

    C. Alfred Hitchcock

    D. Erich von Stroheim

85. He played the role of Winston Churchill in *Inglorious Basterds*.

    A. James Fox

    B. Omar Sharif

    C. Tom Courtenay

    D. Rod Taylor

86. Which real-life commander was the inspiration for the General Frank Savage character in *Twelve O'Clock High*?

    A. Charles Fox

    B. Frank Armstrong

    C. Ira Eaker

    D. Benjamin Foulois

87. In this 1964 thriller, the Nazis kidnap a US Army officer and try to convince him the war is over in order to learn details about the D-Day invasion.

    A. *Night Passage*

    B. *36 Hours*

    C. *The Quiller Memorandum*

    D. *Strangers When We Meet*

88. This motion picture's tagline was "Tougher than Leather ... Harder to Kill!"

    A. *Wake Island*

    B. *Fighting Leathernecks*

    C. *Halls of Montezuma*

    D. *To the Shores of Tripoli*

89. In *The Outsider*, _____ portrayed a Puma Indian who enlisted in the US Marine Corps and was one of six flag raisers on Iwo Jima.

    A. Tony Curtis

    B. Anthony Perkins

    C. Sal Mineo

    D. Robert Vaughn

90. Which *Cheers* cast member made a cameo appearance in *Saving Private Ryan*?

    A. David Hyde Pierce

    B. Kelsey Grammer

    C. Woody Harrelson

    D. Ted Danson

91. John Wayne's character in *Flying Leathernecks* was based on which real-life Medal of Honor recipient?

    A. Captain John Smith

    B. Major Joe Foss

    C. Captain Richard Fleming

    D. Major Gregory Boyington

92. Who played Field Marshal Rommel in *Five Graves to Cairo*?

    A. Erich von Stroheim

    B. James Mason

    C. Conrad Reinhard

    D. Karl Michael Vogler

93. In *A Walk in the Sun*, which of the following actors made his film debut?

    A. Dana Andrews

    B. Lloyd Bridges

    C. John Ireland

    D. Richard Conte

94. This pop artist recorded the soundtrack to the 1968 movie *Anzio*.

    A. Johnny Mathis

    B. Andy Williams

    C. Bobby Vinton

    D. Jack Jones

95. In which film will you find a Sherman tank named "Fury"?

    A. *Raid on Rommel*

    B. *Tobruk*

    C. *Fury*

    D. *Tank Command*

96. On which movie set was actress Mia Farrow introduced to her future husband Frank Sinatra?

    A. *Cast a Giant Shadow*

    B. *The Victors*

    C. *Von Ryan's Express*

    D. *Never So Few*

97. Name the actor who was also a real-life amputee in *The Best Years of Our Lives.*

    A. Ray Collins

    B. Walter Baldwin

    C. Harold Russell

    D. Steve Cochran

98. Which actor killed Ernest Borgnine's character, Sergeant "Fatso" Judson, in *From Here to Eternity*?

    A. Burt Lancaster

    B. Richard Conte

    C. Montgomery Clift

    D. John Garfield

99. He portrayed the commandant of the Plaszow concentration camp in *Schindler's List.*

    A. Ralph Fiennes

    B. Jason Issacs

    C. Liam Neeson

    D. Jude Law

100. This American composer scored such films as *In Harm's Way* and *Patton.*

    A. Nelson Riddle

    B. Elmer Bernstein

    C. Jerry Goldsmith

    D. Aaron Copland

CHAPTER 9 ANSWERS

1. A. *Twelve O'Clock High*

2. B. Audie Murphy

3. B. *Darkest Hour*

4. D. *Saving Private Ryan*

5. B. James Mason

6. C. *Heaven Knows Mr. Allison*

7. C. Wolfgang Preiss

8. C. *Memphis Belle*

9. C. *Das Boot*

10. D. Frank Capra

11. C. Trevor Howard

12. D. Henry Fonda

13. D. George Murphy

14. A. Dimitri Tiomkin

15. C. Burgess Meredith

16. B. *From Here to Eternity*

17. C. Dean Martin

18. D. Jeff Chandler

19. C. *Dunkirk*

20. B. Thirteen

21. A. Cliff Robertson

22. B. Kirk Douglas

23. A. George C. Scott

24. C. *Letters from Iwo Jima*

25. C. Maximilian Schell

26. B. Humphrey Bogart

27. A. *The Gallant Hours*

28. C. Douglas Bader

29. B. Art Garfunkel

30. C. *The Incredible Mr. Limpet*

31. B. *Flying Tigers*

32. C. David Niven

33. C. Alec Guinness

34. C. *Casablanca*

35. C. *Mr. Roberts*

36. A. Ben Kingsley

37. D. *The Heroes of Telemark*

38. B. Triumph TR6 Trophy

39. A. *The Enemy Below*

40. B. *Run Silent Run Deep*

41. C. Charles Bronson

42. B. *Kelly's Heroes*

43. A. *The Thin Red Line*

44. B. Ronald Reagan

45. A. *The Night of the Generals*

46. C. "Tom, Dick, and Harry"

47. C. Otto Preminger

48. A. *Mr. Roberts*

49. A. Richard Burton

50. A. *A Midnight Clear*

51. C. Bobby Darin

52. C. Frederick "Fritz" Niland

53. C. Bob Hoskins

54. B. *Hacksaw Ridge*

55. C. Donald Pleasence

56. A. Clark Gable

57. B. *Patton*

58. B. Delmer Davies

59. D. *The Pianist*

60. B. One

61. C. Cuba Gooding Jr.

62. B. Garth Brooks

63. B. "Lulu Belle"

64. B. Hitler's Berlin bunker

65. B. Tiger! Tiger! Tiger!

66. C. *The Best Years of Our Lives*

67. A. *Shining Through*

68. B. Tom Cruise

69. C. He's a German spy.

70. D. works of art

71. C. Shohei Hino

72. C. *The Eagle Has Landed*

73. A. Bill Murray

74. C. *December*

75. A. Richard Boone and Robert Wagner

76. D. *Battle of the Bulge*

77. C. *Buck Privates*

78. C. Peter Sellers

79. A. Paul Anka

80. C. Sessue Hayakawa

81. B. Paul Newman

82. A. *Sink the Bismarck!*

83. D. Guadalcanal

84. B. Otto Preminger

85. D. Rod Taylor

86. B. Frank Armstrong

87. B. *36 Hours*

88. A. *Wake Island*

89. A. Tony Curtis

90. D. Ted Danson

91. A. Captain John Smith

92. A. Erich von Stroheim

93. C. John Ireland

94. D. Jack Jones

95. C. *Fury*

96. C. *Von Ryan's Express*

97. C. Harold Russell

98. C. Montgomery Clift

99. A. Ralph Fiennes

100. C. Jerry Goldsmith

CHAPTER 10
TELEVISION PROGRAMS

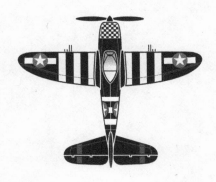

1. Which Oscar-winning actor guest-starred in three episodes of *Combat!*?

    A. Jason Robards

    B. Robert Duvall

    C. Lee Marvin

    D. Sean Connery

2. Paul Burke replaced this actor in the leading role on *Twelve O'Clock High*.

    A. Nick Adams

    B. Robert Lansing

    C. James Franciscus

    D. Clint Eastwood

3. Which cast member on *McHale's Navy* went on to star on *Love Boat*?

    A. Tim Conway

    B. Gavin MacLeod

    C. Bernie Kopell

    D. Harvey Korman

4. The aviator jacket worn by Bob Crane on *Hogan's Heroes* was previously worn by Frank Sinatra in which film?

    A. *Cast a Giant Shadow*

    B. *From Here to Eternity*

    C. *Von Ryan's Express*

    D. *The Manchurian Candidate*

5. Which character on *The Gallant Men* served as the show's narrator?

    A. Captain Jim Benedict

    B. Lieutenant Frank Kimbro

    C. Sergeant John McKenna

    D. Correspondent Conley Wright

6. This was the name of the B-17 flown by Colonel Joe Gallagher on *Twelve O'Clock High*.

    A. *Swamp Ghost*

    B. *The Pink Lady*

    C. *Piccadilly Lily*

    D. None of the above

7. "Hell Was an Ocean Away" was the tagline for this miniseries.

    A. *Pearl*

    B. *The Mighty Eighth*

    C. *The Pacific*

    D. *The Caine Mutiny Court-Martial*

8. Name the short-lived 1950s TV program that explored US submarine operations during World War II.

    A. *Up Periscope!*

    B. *The Silent Service*

    C. *Dive!*

    D. *Sea Hunt*

9. His *Winds of War* and *War and Remembrance* became award-winning miniseries on ABC.

    A. Edwin Hoyt

    B. Herman Wouk

    C. James Jones

    D. David Halberstam

10. In two episodes of *Baa Baa Black Sheep*, real-life fighter ace Pappy Boyington played

    A. General Harrison Kenlay

    B. Major Red Buell

    C. Colonel Robert Gibbons

    D. General Charles Mathis

11. This *Combat!* character carried a BAR.

    A. Littlejohn

    B. Hanley

    C. Kirby

    D. Nelson

12. Which was the name of the Gestapo officer on *Hogan's Heroes*?

    A. Captain Hans Muller

    B. Major Wolfgang Hochstetter

    C. Colonel Josepf Vogel

    D. General Claus Burkhalter

13. This motion picture was the inspiration for the short-lived series *Garrison's Gorillas*.

    A. *Satan's Soldiers*

    B. *The Dirty Devils*

    C. *Sabotage Squad*

    D. *The Dirty Dozen*

14. In *Band of Brothers,* _____ portrayed legendary Colonel Robert F. Sink and served as technical advisor for the miniseries.

    A. Colin Hanks

    B. Dale Dye

    C. Neal McDonough

    D. Tom Hardy

15. Which of the following films was reprised as a TV show?

    A. *Imitation General*

    B. *Francis Joins the WACS*

    C. *Murphy's War*

    D. *The Diary of Anne Frank*

16. He was the narrator of the British-produced series *The World at War.*

    A. Ben Kingsley

    B. Laurence Olivier

    C. Peter O'Toole

    D. Dirk Bogarde

17. This *McHale's Navy* cast member died of an apparent heart attack while swimming in his Beverly Hills pool.

    A.   Ken Ritter

    B.   Gary Vinson

    C.   Billy Sands

    D.   Joe Flynn

18. Who replaced Kinchloe (actor Ivan Dixon) when he left the cast of *Hogan's Heroes* in 1970?

    A.   Tim Reid

    B.   Ron Glass

    C.   Tim Brown

    D.   Kenneth Washington

19. In the 1983 television remake of *Casablanca*, who took the role of Rick?

    A.   Tom Selleck

    B.   Harvey Keitel

    C.   David Soul

    D.   Paul Michael Glaser

20. The tagline for this miniseries was: "They Depended on Each Other. And the World Depended on Them."

    A.   *Pearl*

    B.   *Winds of War*

    C.   *Band of Brothers*

    D.   *From Here to Eternity*

21. Which two members of the *Combat!* cast were nominated for Primetime Emmys?

    A. Rick Jason and Vic Morrow

    B. Pierre Jalbert and Jack Hogan

    C. Vic Morrow and Conlan Carter

    D. Rick Jason and Dick Peabody

22. Before playing an undercover agent on *Blue Light*, this actor/singer starred opposite Julie Andrews and Richard Burton on Broadway in *Camelot*.

    A. Richard Kiley

    B. Steve Lawrence

    C. Hal Linden

    D. Robert Goulet

23. Which character on *The Rat Patrol* was an Englishman?

    A. Private Tully Pettigrew

    B. Sergeant Jack Moffitt

    C. Private Mark Hitchcock

    D. Sergeant Sam Troy

24. Best known for playing Gomez on *The Addams Family*, he also starred in the wartime comedy *Operation Petticoat*.

    A. Larry Hagman

    B. Fred Gwynne

    C. John Astin

    D. Bob Newhart

25. *McHale's Navy* spawned two feature films. What were they?

    A. *McHale's Navy* and *McHale's Navy Joins the Air Force*

    B. *McHale's Navy* and *McHale's Navy Goes to Hollywood*

    C. *McHale's Navy* and *McHale's Navy Joins the Army*

    D. *McHale's Navy* and *McHale's Navy Wins the War*

26. Which late-night talk show host made a cameo appearance in *Band of Brothers*?

    A. Jimmy Fallon

    B. Stephen Colbert

    C. Jimmy Kimmel

    D. Conan O'Brien

27. How many episodes of *Combat!* aired between 1962 and 1967?

    A. 131

    B. 217

    C. 152

    D. 167

28. Oscar-nominated for *12 Years a Slave* and *Steve Jobs*, Michael Fassbender made his acting debut in

    A. *The Pacific*

    B. *Duty, Honor, Country*

    C. *The Winds of War*

    D. *Band of Brothers*

29. Which was the first name of Ernest Borgnine's character on *McHale's Navy*?

   A. Clint

   B. Quinton

   C. Winston

   D. Charles

30. Before playing Private Bernie Lucavich on *The Gallant Men*, Roland La Starza was a(n)

   A. truck driver

   B. housepainter

   C. auto mechanic

   D. prizefighter

31. "The Story of Man's Inhumanity to Man" was the tagline for this miniseries.

   A. *The Pacific*

   B. *Nuremberg*

   C. *Holocaust*

   D. *Colditz*

32. Which character on *The Rat Patrol* wore glasses?

   A. Sergeant Sam Troy

   B. Private Mark Hitchcock

   C. Sergeant Jack Moffitt

   D. Private Tully Pettigrew

33. This actor on *McHale's Navy* was also an accomplished magician.

    A. Ernest Borgnine

    B. Carl Ballantine

    C. Joe Flynn

    D. Edson Stroll

34. Best known for his work in motion pictures, _____ also directed episodes of *Combat!* and *The Gallant Men*.

    A. David Fincher

    B. Robert Altman

    C. John Sturges

    D. Robert Aldrich

35. Which member of the *Friends* cast appeared in three episodes of *Band of Brothers*?

    A. Matt LeBlanc

    B. David Schwimmer

    C. Matthew Perry

    D. James Michael Tyler

36. An unlikely choice, Tom Selleck portrayed General Dwight Eisenhower in this 2004 TV movie.

    A. *Ike: The War Years*

    B. *Eisenhower: Man of Destiny*

    C. *Ike: Countdown to D-Day*

    D. *Eisenhower: Hour of Decision*

37. This actor appeared in the film *The Wackiest Ship in the Army* and as a regular on the TV series of the same name.

    A. Jack Lemmon

    B. Gary Collins

    C. Ricky Nelson

    D. Mike Kellin

38. Which US infantry division is depicted in *The Gallant Men*?

    A. 17th

    B. 25th

    C. 36th

    D. 48th

39. The following shows aired on ABC *except*

    A. *Blue Light*

    B. *Garrison's Gorillas*

    C. *Hogan's Heroes*

    D. *Twelve O'Clock High*

40. A longtime cast member on *The Young and the Restless*, this veteran actor was a regular on *The Rat Patrol*.

    A. Doug Davidson

    B. Peter Bergman

    C. Gary Raymond

    D. Eric Braeden

41. Best known as the charismatic host of *Family Feud*, he also starred on *Hogan's Heroes*.

    A. Bob Eubanks

    B. Ray Combs

    C. Bob Crane

    D. Richard Dawson

42. Who portrayed General Patton in the made-for-TV movie *The Last Days of Patton*?

    A. Gerald McRaney

    B. Stephen McNally

    C. Mitchell Ryan

    D. George C. Scott

43. The following were Captain Binghamton's favorite expressions on *McHale's Navy except*

    A. "McHale, you idiot!"

    B. "I could just scream!"

    C. "Why me? Why is it always me?"

    D. "What is it? What, what, what?"

44. Who played the Deborah Kerr role in the 1979 miniseries *From Here to Eternity*?

    A. Jill St. John

    B. Natalie Wood

    C. Stephanie Powers

    D. Kim Basinger

45. He played the role of Lieutenant Doug Roberts on the TV version of *Mr. Roberts*.

   A.   Troy Donahue

   B.   Grant Williams

   C.   Roger Smith

   D.   Efrem Zimbalist Jr.

46. Which veteran TV actor starred as Major Frank Whittaker in the 1966 series *Court-Martial*?

   A.   Adam West

   B.   William Shatner

   C.   Bradford Dillman

   D.   Peter Graves

47. He played bumbling Ensign Charles Parker on *McHale's Navy*.

   A.   Harvey Korman

   B.   Jim Nabors

   C.   Tim Conway

   D.   None of the above

48. Which member of the boy band, New Kids on the Block, had a starring role in *Band of Brothers*?

   A.   Danny Wood

   B.   Joey McIntyre

   C.   Donnie Wahlberg

   D.   Jordan Miller

49. The tagline for this miniseries was "Brothers in War ... Rivals in Love."

    A. *Colditz*

    B. *Piece of Cake*

    C. *Rolling Thunder*

    D. *War and Remembrance*

50. Which was the first series to originate in color?

    A. *The Rat Patrol*

    B. *Decision before Dawn*

    C. *Twelve O'Clock High*

    D. *Combat!*

51. The POW camp on *Hogan's Heroes* was called

    A. *Stalag* 6

    B. *Stalag* 11

    C. *Stalag* 13

    D. *Stalag* 17

52. Who starred as Captain Jim Benedict on *The Gallant Men* and later played Special Agent Tom Colby on *The FBI*?

    A. William Reynolds

    B. Robert Conrad

    C. Hugh O'Brien

    D. Gene Barry

53. In the 1970s TV movie *The Execution of Private Slovik*, why was Slovik put to death?

    A. He murdered a fellow GI.

    B. He stole $10,000 from a bank.

    C. He deserted his post.

    D. He struck a superior officer.

54. Lieutenant Hanley's first name on *Combat!* was

    A. Sid

    B. Gil

    C. Will

    D. Stu

55. On *Baa Baa Black Sheep*, this was the unit's official designation.

    A. US Army Fighter Squadron 6

    B. US Marine Attack Squadron 17

    C. US Navy Assault Squadron 128

    D. US Marine Attack Squadron 214

56. Which ABC series was loosely based on the exploits of the famed "Red Ball Express"?

    A. *Drive*

    B. *Fast Forward*

    C. *Thunder Alley*

    D. *Roll Out*

57. This city was the setting for *Goodtime Girls*.

    A. London, England

    B. Minneapolis, Minnesota

    C. Washington, DC

    D. Las Vegas, Nevada

58. In *Ike: The War Years*, who played the role of Eisenhower's driver and personal secretary Kay Summersby?

    A. Jane Fonda

    B. Lee Remick

    C. Elizabeth Taylor

    D. Helen Mirren

59. He was the only actor on *Hogan's Heroes* to win two Primetime Emmys.

    A. John Banner

    B. Bob Crane

    C. Werner Klemperer

    D. Robert Clary

60. On *Danger UXB*, Lieutenant Brian Ash (Anthony Andrews)

    A. deactivated bombs

    B. assassinated enemy agents

    C. flew bomber missions

    D. commanded a tank battalion

61. He played the title character on *Foyle's War*.

    A. Kenneth Branagh

    B. Michael Kitchen

    C. Arthur Lowe

    D. Michael Caine

62. Which member of the *Combat!* squad spoke French?

    A. Doc

    B. Lemay

    C. Nelson

    D. Kirby

63. Veteran actor Jack Warden played a US Army officer on this show.

    A. *The Wackiest Ship in the Army*

    B. *Operation Petticoat*

    C. *The Wackiest Ship in the Navy*

    D. *Combat Command*

64. Which former *Saturday Night Live* cast member was a regular on *Roll Out*?

    A. Chris Rock

    B. Eddie Murphy

    C. Garrett Morris

    D. Michael Che

65. How many episodes of *McHale's Navy* aired during its four-year run?

    A. 84

    B. 97

    C. 111

    D. 138

66. Which was the sequel to the BBC series *Secret War*?

    A. *Foyle's War*

    B. *Wish Me Luck*

    C. *Kessler*

    D. *Colditz*

67. John Ratzenberger of *Cheers* fame made his TV debut on this program.

    A. *Secret War*

    B. *Pathfinders*

    C. *Jenny's War*

    D. *Dirty Dozen: The Series*

68. The following books were the basis for *The Pacific* except

    A. *Helmet for My Pillow*

    B. *Pacific Crucible*

    C. *Red Blood, Black Sand*

    D. *With the Old Breed*

69. Which of the following miniseries became a weekly program on NBC?

    A. *The Undefeated*

    B. *What Price Glory*

    C. *From Here to Eternity*

    D. None of the above

70. On *Twelve O'Clock High*, the unit's official designation was the

    A. 132nd Fighter Group

    B. 227th Bombardment Group

    C. 329th Fighter Group

    D. 918th Bombardment Group

71. The tagline for this miniseries was "Fierce. Unexpected. The Day That Changed Everything."

    A. *Colditz*

    B. *Pearl*

    C. *A Town Like Alice*

    D. *Struggles with Miller*

72. Which BBC series focused on female POWs in a Japanese internment camp?

    A. *Wish Me Luck*

    B. *Nancy Wake*

    C. *The Last Bastion*

    D. *Tenko*

73. In *The Last Days of Patton*, who portrayed General Dwight Eisenhower?

    A. Richard Dysart

    B. Murray Hamilton

    C. Victor Jouet

    D. Charles Lane

74. Which star from *Colditz* played Major Dick Winters in *Band of Brothers*?

    A. Ron Livingston

    B. Tom Hardy

    C. Damien Lewis

    D. Mitchell Wilson

75. "Batten Down the Hatches" was the tagline for this program.

    A. *McHale's Navy*

    B. *Voyage to the Bottom of the Sea*

    C. *Down Periscope*

    D. *Operation Petticoat*

76. Which TV show had characters named "Happy" and "Tinker"?

    A. *Navy Log*

    B. *Jericho*

    C. *McHale's Navy*

    D. *Manhunt*

77. In this made-for-TV movie, Ben Gazzara commanded a hard-luck US division following D-Day.

    A. *Fast Forward*

    B. *Fireball Forward*

    C. *Diamond Forward*

    D. *Lucky Forward*

78. Which composer wrote the theme song for *Hogan's Heroes*?

    A. Jack Eliot

    B. Ray Evans

    C. Charles Fox

    D. Jerry Fielding

79. This was the name of the PT base on *McHale's Navy*.

    A. Shangri-La

    B. Taratupa

    C. Pogo Pogo

    D. Mystic Cove

80. Which of the following TV shows aired on NBC?

    A. *O.S.S.*

    B. *Spyforce*

    C. *The Underground Front*

    D. None of the above

81. Ron Harper, the star of *Garrison's Gorillas*, was an Ivy League graduate. Which school did he attend?

    A. Dartmouth

    B. Penn

    C. Harvard

    D. Princeton

82. Which was Sergeant Saunders's favorite expression on *Combat!*?

    A. "Kirby, not on your life!"

    B. "Let's do it!"

    C. "Littlejohn, keep quiet!"

    D. "Take the point!"

83. This wartime drama featured characters with names such as "Casino" and "Chief."

    A. *The Gallant Men*

    B. *Garrison's Gorillas*

    C. *Baa Baa Black Sheep*

    D. *The Conquerors*

84. Which composer scored both *The Rat Patrol* and *Twelve O'Clock High*?

    A. Dominic Frontiere

    B. George Greeley

    C. Ernest Gold

    D. Howard Greenfield

85. This future star of the film *M*A*S*H* appeared in five different episodes of *Twelve O'Clock High* playing five different roles.

    A. Donald Sutherland

    B. Elliot Gould

    C. Gary Burghoff

    D. Tom Skerritt

86. On *Hogan's Heroes*, which name does Colonel Hogan use when communicating with Allied headquarters?

    A. "Mickey Mouse"

    B. "Goldilocks"

    C. "Donald Duck"

    D. "Papa Bear"

87. Before being appointed US ambassador to Mexico by President Ronald Reagan, John Gavin played the skipper of a US destroyer on this show.

    A. *Convoy*

    B. *Depth Charge*

    C. *Away All Boats!*

    D. *Task Force*

88. On *The Rat Patrol*, this was Sergeant Troy's favorite expression.

    A. "Head out!"

    B. "Let's roll!"

    C. "Mount up and move out!"

    D. "Let's shake it!"

89. Which two original cast members from the film *The Dirty Dozen* also appeared in the 1987 TV movie *The Dirty Dozen: The Deadly Mission*?

    A. Lee Marvin and Robert Ryan

    B. Charles Bronson and Donald Sutherland

    C. Telly Savalas and Ernest Borgnine

    D. Trini Lopez and Clint Walker

90. A onetime musical director for Frank Sinatra, he wrote the theme to *McHale's Navy*.

    A. Gordon Jenkins

    B. Axle Stordahl

    C. Nelson Riddle

    D. Billy May

91. Who scored the music for *Blue Light*?

    A. John Williams

    B. Robert Cobert

    C. Lalo Schifrin

    D. Joe Harnell

92. This was Sergeant Schultz's favorite catchphrase on *Hogan's Heroes*.

    A. "What me?"

    B. "I know nothing; I see nothing!"

    C. "May I have one more piece of pie?"

    D. "Over my dead body!"

93. Who portrayed Colonel Pappy Boyington on *Baa Baa Black Sheep*?

    A.   William Conrad

    B.   Dana Elcar

    C.   Robert Conrad

    D.   Simon Oakland

94. On *Twelve O'Clock High*, which was Major Harvey Stovall's profession before the war?

    A.   Lawyer

    B.   Accountant

    C.   Surgeon

    D.   College professor

95. In which country did *Bomb Girls* take place?

    A.   Germany

    B.   United States

    C.   Italy

    D.   Canada

96. The tagline for this short-lived TV series was "Nobody Understands the True Cost of War Better Than Women."

    A.   *Jenny's War*

    B.   *Goodtime Girls*

    C.   *Dad's Army*

    D.   *Home Fires*

97. Which actor played the leading role on *The Dirty Dozen: The Television Series*?

    A. Dak Miller

    B. Brian Walker

    C. Ben Murphy

    D. Marv Preston

98. He was the executive producer of the 2007 PBS documentary series *The War*.

    A. Michael Burns

    B. Paul Devlin

    C. Ross McElwee

    D. Ken Burns

99. This was the name of Colonel Klink's first secretary on *Hogan's Heroes*.

    A. Olga

    B. Helga

    C. Gilda

    D. Hilda

100. Which English city was the setting for *A Family at War*?

    A. Liverpool

    B. Manchester

    C. Bristol

    D. Leeds

CHAPTER 10 ANSWERS

1. B. Robert Duvall

2. B. Robert Lansing

3. B. Gavin MacLeod

4. C. *Von Ryan's Express*

5. D. Correspondent Conley Wright

6. C. *Piccadilly Lily*

7. C. *The Pacific*

8. B. *The Silent Service*

9. B. Herman Wouk

10. A. General Harrison Kenlay

11. C. Kirby

12. B. Major Wolfgang Hochstetter

13. D. *The Dirty Dozen*

14. B. Dale Dye

15. D. *The Diary of Anne Frank*

16. B. Laurence Olivier

17. D. Joe Flynn

18. D. Kenneth Washington

19. C. David Soul

20. C. *Band of Brothers*

21. C. Vic Morrow and Conlan Carter

22. D. Robert Goulet

23. B. Sergeant Jack Moffitt

24. C. John Astin

25. A. *McHale's Navy* and *McHale's Navy Joins the Air Force*

26. A. Jimmy Fallon

27. C. 152

28. D. *Band of Brothers*

29. B. Quinton

30. D. prizefighter

31. C. *Holocaust*

32. B. Private Mark Hitchcock

33. B. Carl Ballantine

34. B. Robert Altman

35. B. David Schwimmer

36. C. *Ike: Countdown to D-Day*

37. D. Mike Kellin

38. C. 36th

39. C. *Hogan's Heroes*

40. D. Eric Braeden

41. D. Richard Dawson

42. D. George C. Scott

43. A. "McHale, you idiot!"

44. B. Natalie Wood

45. C. Roger Smith

46. D. Peter Graves

47. C. Tim Conway

48. C. Donnie Wahlberg

49. A. *Colditz*

50. A. *The Rat Patrol*

51. C. *Stalag* 13

52. A. William Reynolds

53. C. He deserted his post.

54. B. Gil

55. D. US Marine Attack Squadron 214

56. D. *Roll Out*

57. C. Washington, DC

58. B. Lee Remick

59. C. Werner Klemperer

60. A. deactivated bombs

61. B. Michael Kitchen

62. B. Lemay

63. A. *The Wackiest Ship in the Army*

64. C. Garrett Morris

65. D. 138

66. C. *Kessler*

67. A. *Secret War*

68. B. *Pacific Crucible*

69. C. *From Here to Eternity*

70. D. 918th Bombardment Group

71. B. *Pearl*

72. D. *Tenko*

73. A. Richard Dysart

74. C. Damien Lewis

75. A. *McHale's Navy*

76. C. *McHale's Navy*

77. B. *Fireball Forward*

78. D. Jerry Fielding

79. B. Taratupa

80. D. None of the above

81. D. Princeton

82. D. "Take the point!"

83. B. *Garrison's Gorillas*

84. A. Dominic Frontiere

85. D. Tom Skerritt

86. B. "Goldilocks"

87. A. *Convoy*

88. D. "Let's shake it!"

89. C. Telly Savalas and Ernest Borgnine

90. B. Axle Stordahl

91. C. Lalo Schifrin

92. B. "I know nothing; I see nothing!"

93. C. Robert Conrad

94. A. Lawyer

95. D. Canada

96. D. *Home Fires*

97. C. Ben Murphy

98. D. Ken Burns

99. B. Helga

100. A. Liverpool